WAR OR REVOLUTION

WAR OR REVOLUTION

Russian Jews and Conscription in Britain, 1917

HAROLD SHUKMAN

To Zahava and Ralph
with best wishes
from the author's son
David

VALLENTINE MITCHELL
LONDON • PORTLAND, OR

First published in 2006 in Great Britain by
VALLENTINE MITCHELL
Suite 314, Premier House, 112–114 Station Road,
Edgware, Middlesex HA8 7BJ

and in the United States of America by
VALLENTINE MITCHELL
c/o ISBS, 920 NE 58th Avenue, Suite 300
Portland, OR 97213-3786

Website: http://www.vm.books.com

British Library Cataloguing in Publication Data
Shukman, Harold
    War or revolution : Russian Jews and conscription in
    Britain, 1917
    1.Russia. Armiia – Recruiting, enlistment, etc – World
    War, 1914–1918 2.Jews, Russian – Great Britain – History –
    20th century 3.World War, 1914–1918 – Russia –
    Participation, Jewish 4.World War, 1914–1918 – Soviet Union –
    Participation, Jewish 5.World War, 1914–1918 – Campaigns
    – Russia 6.World War, 1914–1918 – Campaigns – Soviet Union
    I. Title
    940.4'03'0947

ISBN 0-85303-707-8 (cloth)
ISBN 0-85303-708-6 (paper)

Library of Congress Cataloging-in-Publication Data
A catalog record has been applied for

Typeset in 11/13pt Sabon by FiSH Books, Enfield, Middx
Printed in Great Britain by MPG Books Ltd, Bodmin, Cornwall

For my wife Barbara

Contents

List of Plates

Prologue

On a stormy September afternoon in 1917, a long, bedraggled procession of Jewish men trudged through the streets of East London to King's Cross Station. Having arrived only a few years before as refugees from the pogroms and oppression of Tsarist Russia, they were now on their way back to serve in what, a few months earlier, was known as the Imperial Russian Army. Or would have done, had the Bolshevik Revolution not happened within weeks of their reaching Russia. An eye-witness recalled: 'Clutching sandwiches wrapped in newspaper and their cardboard suitcases, these men had the lost look of a crowd unable to move except where directed. But while some wept, others looked relieved, and joked among themselves. Wives had to remain behind ... Some of these women would never see their husbands again.' The men boarded a train for Liverpool where ships were waiting to take them – and soon another 3,000 of them – to the Arctic wastes of northern Russia and into the chaos of Revolution and Civil War.

An agreement – 'The Convention' – between the British and Russian governments had caught these 'friendly aliens' in a web of obligation to fight in their armies, and a choice had been offered: serve in the British Army or go back to Russia and fight there. They had made their choice, and they were now beginning to live with its consequences. They would all see action, though not necessarily military, and they would all experience extraordinary odysseys in the turmoil of the ensuing years, as they sought desperately to return to the families they had left behind in England.

Among the men plodding through the heavy summer rain towards King's Cross – but from the *West* End – was my father, David Shukman. He had come to London in 1913. Now aged 37, with two small children and a wife who was about to produce a third, like many of his comrades that day he was no stranger to war, and his strong desire to avoid this one was not from cowardice. He had spent four years in the Russian Army – a hazardous occupation even in peacetime – eighteen months of it in Manchuria during the Russo-Japanese War. His discharge book shows that he had fought in the 1905 Battle of Mukden, in which nearly 400,000 Russian troops engaged with over 200,000 Japanese – together the greatest assembly of force in the history of war until then, and one of the bloodiest. He, and many like him, had recoiled from repeating on the Western Front what rumour suggested was an even bloodier conflict.

During his military service David had been posted to Simferopol in the Crimea and, finding life after demobilisation back home in a tiny *shtetl* (Jewish townlet or village) too restricted, and even after giving Warsaw a try, he retraced his steps to the sunny south. There, in 1910, he married my mother, Manya, and three years later they set up home in London, north of Soho in what today is loftily dubbed Fitzrovia, a short walk of a mile and a half from King's Cross Station.

Of the 120,000 Russian Jewish immigrants who had settled in Britain over the previous thirty-odd years, about 30,000 men were eligible for military service. Half of these somehow managed to slip through the bureaucratic net. Of the remainder, about 4,000 joined the British Army, a similar number were excused on medical grounds, others because they were doing war work. The rest, known as the Conventionists, had to make the journey of return to the very country they had so recently fled. This book tells their story.

1 The Idea of Conscription

When the Great War broke out in August 1914, of all the belligerents only Britain did not have a system of conscription. Britain's allies, Russia and France, like their common enemies Germany, Austria-Hungary and the Ottoman Empire, were able to launch total mobilisation within hours of the declaration of war, since their compulsory military service arrangements were of long standing, well tried and universal in scope. By contrast, Britain relied on volunteers to swell the ranks of her small standing army of regulars, and it was not until May 1916, nearly two years into the war, that conscription for all able-bodied men between the ages of 18 and 41 was finally introduced.

Resistance to compulsory military service derived from many sources, emotional and objective, and social historians have done much to chart these foggy reaches for students of the First World War who may wander in from other fields. To the student of Russian history, for example, it comes as a surprise to learn that resistance to military service in Britain outlived not only the patriotic upsurge at the beginning of the war, but even the armistice and the years of peace that followed. The objection to conscription had deep social roots that pre-existed the war and were not materially affected by the course of its outcome. In Russia, evasion rather than objection had long been a familiar if more barbaric practice, with harrowing accounts of self-mutilation by conscripts desperate to escape the torments of service in the Tsar's army – twenty-five years, until the reforms of 1874 reduced it to six and then four. Conscription was opposed in Britain because it was seen to conflict with the voluntary principle as one of the hallmarks of an Englishman's (Scotsman's, Irishman's, Welshman's) liberty, his freedom to choose to go and not to be dragooned or dragged into the trenches, his freedom to die for his country.

The patriotic upsurge at the outbreak of the war was common to all the Allies, where men of all classes flocked to the colours in the belief that the cause was just and that the war would be short, 'over by Christmas'. In 1914, then, the Allies were finding the manpower, whether as in France and Russia by means of universal conscription or as in Britain by voluntary enlistment. Britain's supply of manpower soon began to slow down, however, and the question of compulsion began to be seriously debated, for the first time since it was raised in the Boer War of 1899–1902.

Britain did not have conscription and therefore did not have a large standing army. Britain's wars had all been abroad and (until 1899) of small scale, and small professional armies had proved sufficient for the purpose. Apart from India, which evolved its own military structures under British rule, Britain's military presence in her overseas possessions performed custodial and police functions, rather than offensive or defensive roles for which much larger forces would have been needed. As for Britain's own defence needs, they were served by her powerful navy, the proper defender of an island state.

In addition, the English liberal tradition had imbued an aversion to large standing armies as potential instruments of tyranny. In Britain the profession of soldier was not held in high esteem – that much at least he had in common with his Russian comrades, who were excluded from theatres, restaurants and the interior of trams; public parks in Russian cities had large signs which read 'Dogs and soldiers forbidden to enter'. The outbreak of the war naturally put a strain on English objections to conscription and, as time went on and as Christmas 1914 came and went, the argument from principle had to contend with glaring facts in favour of expediency.

Every week for the first three months of the war an average of 75,000 men volunteered, about nine times the number the government had expected. The army could not properly accommodate so many, nor find them uniforms, nor, most important, the weapons to arm them. Stories had filtered through to the British government that Russia, with its controlled recruitment, also lacked weapons for its millions, that while three men peered over the top firing their rifles, another seven were being ordered to sit in the trench and clap their hands to imitate the noise of gunfire. Voluntarism, like compulsion, needed intelligent planning, a rational ordering which in Britain was done by tightening up recruiting standards, rather than resorting to conscription. By the end of 1914 the flow had fallen to 30,000 a week.

The voluntary campaign had other costs of which the Liberal

government soon became aware. In its indiscriminate absorption of manpower it had accepted men of every description, educated and uneducated, skilled and unskilled, men who might make a better contribution to the war effort by working in a munitions factory rather than the trenches. This argument was used in the War Cabinet against those opponents of conscription who feared that its universality would have the same disastrous effect in industry as voluntarism: conscription was planned to be based not on blind egalitarianism, but on the rational principle of judicious exemption for those of special value to the war effort.

With the slow-down of volunteers and the growing awareness that the war was not going to end soon, the pro-conscription lobby in the British government gained ground. Against those who feared conscription as a possible trigger of popular disorder it was argued that the public was becoming impatient with able-bodied young men dodging the war at home while their more patriotic fathers were fighting in the trenches.

The emotional atmosphere surrounding the issue of conscription had done much to slow down its introduction. It had been advocated from the start by the 'jingoists' – 'hawks' in today's jargon. For them there should be no pussyfooting debate about an Englishman's duty to serve his country. All the arguments for voluntarism and conscientious objection were swept aside in the all-out patriotic fervour of the popular press which lambasted 'shirkers' and 'skrimshankers', reviving the worst features of the white-feather campaign of the Boer War. As the government edged slowly towards conscription it was accused by its opponents among the Liberals and Socialists of selling out to the jingoists. Lloyd George, himself an advocate of conscription, concludes in his memoirs that it was only when the successful voluntary campaign – 4,760,000 men by 25 May 1916 – had run its course, that compulsion was adopted by a government that was emotionally hostile to it, and that even the Conservative opposition had not pressed.

In July 1915 parliament passed the National Registration Bill under which all persons between the ages of 15 and 65 were to be registered. The aim was to regulate manpower for military and industrial use. As the Local Government Boards received completed registration forms, men of military age and those in essential work were separately listed. The National Register appeased the opponents of conscription who had feared its wasteful effects on the rational use of manpower, since its purpose was to enable the government to promote the most efficient allocation of men between industry's needs and those of the army. It aroused the hostility of left-wing labour elements who saw it as a convenient mechanism for the early introduction of conscription, and it was above all the Left in British politics that was as hostile to compulsion as it was to the war that was consuming workers' lives.

The registration revealed a total of five million men of military age who were not yet serving, and, after allowing for the medically unfit and those in essential jobs, the figure came down to just below two million. The government now knew that it could not satisfy the army's needs by voluntary recruitment, and the question of either cutting the target or introducing conscription had to be faced. The Cabinet was divided between those who wanted to bring in conscription right away, those who were dead against it and would resign rather than compromise their convictions, and those who were not against it but preferred to wait until it was an absolute necessity, and then only if the mass of the people accepted it.

In one last great effort to bring in volunteers the government launched the Derby Scheme. In October 1915 every British-born man between 18 and 41 on the National Register was asked 'to attest', that is, to pledge himself to go when called, on the understanding that they would all be divided into two classes, married and unmarried, and into 23 groups by age, that the first to be called would be the youngest single men, and that no married men would be called until all the unmarried men had been processed. Married men's doubts were allayed by the promise that if the single men 'hung back', the married men's attestation would not be enforced. All means would be used to conscript the younger men first and the scheme was to be completed by mid-December 1915.

Having received all these assurances, married men attested in large numbers, but only half the single men did so, and so many of them turned out to be medically unfit or in reserved occupations that, out of a possible total of 2,179,231, the net crop of the Derby Scheme came to no more than 343,386, or 16 per cent. Over one million single men had simply refused to attest, in the clear belief that attestation would come to the same thing as volunteering and that once they had become enmeshed in the government machinery they would have no way out. Friendly, or Allied, aliens were not required to sign the National Register nor to attest under the Derby

Scheme. Resistance to recruitment was still a purely home-grown phenomenon.

Conscription was brought closer by the demand of the married men that the government keep its promise not to recruit them in default of the single men who were 'lying low'. In January 1916 Prime Minister Asquith introduced the Military Service Bill under which all single men and widowers between 18 and 41 and without dependants were compelled to attest. The Home Secretary, Sir John Simon, resigned on the principle of opposition to any form of conscription. He was succeeded by Herbert Samuel, an English Jew who played a crucial part in the forthcoming campaign to enlist Russian Jews as 'friendly aliens'. Opposition came from the Liberals in the Cabinet and the Independent Labour Party, which voiced the view of the Left in general. The Bill nevertheless became law on 27 January 1916: all single men and married men aged between 19 and 27 who had not joined up by 1 March would be automatically classified as enlisted men and treated accordingly.

On 21 March the Chief of the Imperial General Staff, General Sir William Robertson, reported to the Cabinet that, out of the nearly 200,000 men called up under the January Military Service Act, 30 per cent had failed to appear. On 3 May, with all the arguments against it overwhelmed by the combination of casualties at the front and evasion at home, the Prime Minister finally grasped the nettle and undertook to impose general and immediate compulsory military service. The Act received the Royal Assent on 25 May 1916.

Between the outbreak of the war in August 1914 and the introduction of conscription in May 1916, nearly five million men had volunteered. The scale of this steady support for the war effort by the British people had clearly given heart to those who were opposed to compulsion. But even when it had been made clear that the country would have to resort to modified compulsion in the form of attestation, young Englishmen in their hundreds of thousands had not come forward, but had preferred social stigma to the horrors they believed lay in store for them on the other side of the Channel. Knowledge of the carnage of the Western Front reached from the War Cabinet down to all levels of society, especially to the men who expected to become 'cannon fodder'. Given the common belief that the average expectation of life for men in the trenches was as little as two weeks, the fall in volunteer numbers is easy to understand.

On 29 June 1916 Herbert Samuel announced unexpectedly that

'alien friends' living in England should either serve in the British Army or return to serve in their 'home countries'. He added that arrangements had already been made with France (an exaggeration, since a formal Anglo-French Convention would not be signed until October 1917), Belgium and Italy, but not yet with Russia. Samuel went on to say that the War Office had 'some time ago' agreed that such men should be regarded as eligible for the British Army. 'We cannot impose compulsion', he conceded, 'but these men are being invited to enlist and many are'. But many were not, and it was these who were to be offered the choice of serving in Britain or going back to Russia. Asked if they would be deported if they refused, Samuel replied, 'I do not put it quite so crudely as that'. There was to be no 'naked threat' of deportation, but nor was it being ruled out as the final sanction.

Very few members of parliament showed much interest in this issue, though those who did came from widely differing positions. In July 1916, for example, the Liberal Joseph King declared that the French government was allowing Russians in France, who were mostly Jewish or political refugees, to emigrate to America, and he wanted to know if the British government was willing to do the same for Russian subjects in this country, if only to harmonise policy with its ally. The Foreign Office pleaded ignorance and gave no opinion. King then asked the Home Secretary what he had in mind for Russian Jews in England, to which Samuel replied that Russians of military age would be required to serve in the British Army, unless they wished to go back to Russia for military service there.

The policy, then, was that Russian Jews should join the British Army, with the stress laid on enlistment, not deportation. This distinction was important, since the Russian Jews thought that *unless* they went back to Russia to join up, they would have to go into the British Army. The British government was not keen to start transporting back to Russia large numbers of unwilling men at a time when there was an acute shipping shortage, and when the North Sea passage to Russia was a dangerous route, dogged by German submarines whose aim was precisely to weaken Russia's war effort. As for the Russian government, it had not asked for the return of these men: what did it want with hostile Jews or organised revolutionaries? There was also the question of caring for the men's dependents once they had been shipped off to Russia. In short, the British government felt it would be in everyone's best interest if the

Russian Jews simply joined up where they were and took the same treatment as everyone else who shared their lot.

The threat of deportation was nevertheless in the minds of both sides – the government's and the refugees'. Once the government had decided it was possible to apply coercion and even deportation for men who did not wish to join the British Army, the scheme acquired an urgency that far outweighed its military significance. Neither the shipping shortage nor the dangers of the route to northern Russia were allowed to stand in the way of transporting a few thousand men of unknown fighting ability into a military environment where nobody could be sure they would even be used for the purpose intended.

Later in July, and at the same time as Lord Sheffield, another friend of the Left, made a similar speech in the House of Lords, Joseph King reminded the Commons that months earlier he had asked whether aliens would be allowed to join the army and hold the King's commission, and for months he had been told they could do neither. Now that conscription was introduced the situation was different. The Home Secretary had suddenly announced the policy of going to the friendly aliens, King went on, and threatening them with deportation if they did not join up. 'You don't get people to join up by threatening them. There has been no press campaign or proper publicity to let them know that they may join the army, and suddenly you descend on them with a threat. Do our Allies approve of this policy?' King conceded that the French government had given its approval to the British policy of sending Frenchmen of military age home to serve in the French Army, ditto Belgian émigrés. 'But with the Russians, Italians, Serbians, Japanese and Portuguese, you haven't been asked by any of them to deport their citizens for military service. In the Russian and Italian cases there is no necessity or desire. What they want is money and munitions, they have plenty of men.' Coming to the crux of the matter, he went on: 'In the case of the Russians, the situation is even more difficult. Most of the Russians here are Jews, who have come mostly through the unfortunate political and social disabilities suffered in Russia and through actual religious persecution. They come here for refuge and asylum.'

King's campaign in parliament was part of a system of peace politics that embraced the question of asylum from a broader point of view. It involved the British Socialist Party, Russian Social Democrats of different kinds, and a range of Russian and Jewish revolutionary-minded bodies. Their common task, at least on the surface, was to protect Russian political exiles and Jews living in Britain, whether as refugees or immigrants, 'protection' meaning from the danger of deportation back to Russia. Since Herbert Samuel had in effect chosen to link the question of compulsory military service with that of deportation, the issue of conscription became enmeshed with that of asylum.

Military service for Russian Jews also became a matter of concern for the Anglo-Jewish community, who feared, with justification, that the reluctance of the Russian Jews to serve their adopted country would have a bad effect on their own good name as loyal subjects. Moves were made in high places by Leopold de Rothschild, Sir Joseph Sebag-Montefiore and other influential figures, with Lucien Wolf, a journalist-cum-lobbyist acting as an intermediary. Committees were formed with the aim of securing for the Russian Jews the most favourable conditions for their entry into the army or exemption from service. Among other things, a promise of easy naturalisation was negotiated, though the files of the British Board of Jewish Deputies contain many cases of Russian Jews who were denied the privilege, despite having fulfilled the requirements.

The Zionists were equally interested in the outcome. In July 1916 the chairman of the Zionist Federation, Chaim Weitzmann, assured a Zionist Conference that an Allied victory would favour their goal of a National Home, adding that he had demanded that nobody should be sent back to Russia and that naturalisation should be granted immediately on entry into the British Army. The role the Jews played in the war in general was seen by the Zionists as an important factor in any post-war settlement. With this same aim, a scheme was in the making to mobilise Jews, of Russian or other origin, in a separate military formation, or Jewish Legion, to fight against Turkey in the Middle East, where it was expected the Jewish National Home would be established.

Joseph King put the case for the Russian Jews on several levels.

First, their economic value: they were largely engaged in producing either uniforms or ammunition boxes for the army and were thus already making a valuable contribution to the war effort; they did not take jobs from anyone, but rather created jobs for others.

Second, on a practical plane, the journey to Archangel close to the Arctic Circle and the only possible point of disembarkation in Russia, was long and hazardous, and Archangel was far from any place of military training, and would involve three or four weeks of travel.

Having dealt with the tangible factors, King then advertised the Jews to the House as simply a good thing: 'Of course, it is one of the basic facts of our history and of other lands that the influx of a Jewish population is always to the benefit of the country to which they have come. Look at this House! Twenty MPs, two Cabinet members, ten with titles. Take any twenty MPs and try and get the same record of achievement. That shows what folly it is, what cruel folly, to embark on a policy that will set the Jewish world, and especially the Jewish immigrant, against the government.' What the Anglo-Jewish establishment – bankers and businessmen – thought about being lumped together with the poorest immigrants – tailors and street traders – can only be imagined.

The solution proposed by King was formulated by the Rothschild committee, together with the War Office, the Russian Committee, which included the leaders of the Zionist Federation, and Lucien Wolf as a mediator, and was known as Herbert Samuel's Scheme B. This was an attempt to reconcile the fears of the English and Russian Jews with the British government's determination that able-bodied Russian Jews of military age should serve. Wolf's name first arose in May 1916, when the Foreign Office informed him of a scheme that had been submitted to the War Office by the Russian Zionist, Vladimir Jabotinsky, proposing that the Russian Jews be offered the opportunity to join a purely Jewish regiment – an old pals' company with no language or other cultural barriers – as a more attractive alternative to the British Army as such. Certain in his own mind that it was hopeless to try to recruit the Russian Jews for the Tsar, Jabotinsky made his appeal directly to the masses themselves, speaking in beautiful Odessa Yiddish. His eloquent soapbox speeches to the reluctant heroes of the East End were greeted with equally eloquent cries of 'War monger!' and 'Capitalist lackey!'

Wolf actually agreed with the line taken by the Home Secretary and privately he deplored the 'unwise and discreditable attitude' taken by the Russian Jews, which he feared could compromise the work of his own Conjoint Committee in aid of the oppressed Jews of Eastern Europe. He nevertheless collaborated in trying to improve the service conditions for the Russian Jews. On 27 July 1916, he had seen Gregory Benenson, a Russian-Jewish magnate, whose daughter Flora Benenson Solomon was an activist in the movement to protect the rights of Russians in England. Benenson had made his fortune in the oil industry in Baku, then, moving to St Petersburg after 1905 he had expanded his interests in gold mining and real estate, and founded the Anglo-Russian Bank. In London since the outbreak of the war, he had created the Russian Jews' Protection Committee (referred to as the Russian Committee). He told Wolf that the situation in the East End among the poorer Russian Jews was deplorable and could become more serious. The problem, Benenson believed, arose because the Russian Jews were very badly informed about the British government's real intentions, and also because they had no reputable leaders of their own whom they could trust. They were bitterly hostile to the War Services Committee, which Leopold de Rothschild had set up to deal with their military service problem, no doubt because they saw it as an agent of the government, which in a sense it was. A new committee was needed to act as intermediary between the government and this particular group of Russian subjects who happened to be Jews, as Wolf put it. For Wolf and Benenson, the starting point of any new arrangements must be the committee's frank acceptance of the liability of the Russian Jews to military service, and the committee's work should be to try to gain concessions from the government, if possible along the lines already being contemplated by the Home Secretary.

With the backing of Sir Joseph Sebag-Montefiore, Leopold de Rothschild and the Home Secretary, Wolf then advised Benenson to get the support of his Russian Zionist friends, Weitzmann and Sokolov, 'who by their silence so far had led the East End to imagine that they were in sympathy with the anti-service party'. Weitzmann and Sokolov agreed to join the committee, opening with a demand to delete any reference to deportation. Wolf objected that without deportation there would be no compulsion, and without compulsion there would be no enlistment. Benenson regarded talk of deportation as an unnecessary irritant. Wolf conceded that it might be sensible to keep it in reserve until they saw the results of the voluntary enlistment scheme, and then passed on the committee's proposals to Herbert Samuel. After a meeting of department heads, Samuel next day told a deputation from the committee that he was willing to make the concessions Wolf had asked for. Benenson then made funds available to open an office in the East End to provide information and propaganda. As for the West End community, it was assumed to be able to keep itself informed by the grapevine.

The scheme announced by Herbert Samuel on 23 August 1916 made no mention of deportation, but stated that further measures would be considered if voluntary enlistment proved unsuccessful. Russian Jews of military age would have until 30 September, about a month from Samuel's announcement, and coercion would not be used until about two weeks after that. As a further concession, in the event of a recruit being killed or dying while in the army, his widow and infant children would have the same right of naturalisation as he would have had. This implied that the government had decided against automatic naturalisation at this stage. Finally, exemptions would operate as they did in Russia.

Wolf wrote to de Rothschild that he found the scheme a generous one that would remove any remaining excuses for the anti-service agitation in the East End. But he was still pessimistic about the outcome: 'The East End people really do not want concessions. What they want is unconditional exemption.' He thought that the War Office was minded to draft all the Russian Jews into labour battalions 'and not send them to the front at all, but, of course, this is a concession which cannot be published'. If that intention had been published and the Russian Jews been told that they were not going to the front after all, the whole picture would surely have changed. As it was, Herbert Samuel expressed his doubts to Wolf: 'If the Committee's propaganda fails, and the mass of the Russian Jews in this country absolutely refuses to lift a finger to help … the effect on the reputation of the Jewish name everywhere will be disastrous.'

The Russian Committee meanwhile was not functioning harmoniously. Montefiore confided to Samuel that Benenson abused the Zionists, Wolf irritated the Russians and the Russians, he suggested, ought to be put in direct contact with King: 'It should make him love them less!' With only one month left to the deadline, it seemed that the Russian Committee was neither positive nor forceful enough in its propaganda in favour of enlistment, and by 6 September Wolf was able to describe it as 'abortive'.

To bolster the Committee's efforts, Leopold de Rothschild and Lord Swaythling published a letter in the Yiddish press on 4 October urging all Russian-Jewish men of military age to recognise their debt of gratitude to England, 'which had given them a generous welcome, security for their persons, schools for their children, and the same opportunities as those enjoyed by Englishmen themselves'. If they joined the British Army every effort would be made to allow them to observe Jewish laws and customs, and to group Jews in batches proportionally. In pay, pensions and promotion they would be treated as native Englishmen, and those who wished to could become naturalised as soon as possible after entering the ranks, without paying the customary fee of £5. And they were given a choice of either enlisting right away or showing their goodwill by registering, a step that would entitle them to apply later on for exemption under the normal conditions. The voluntary scheme would now be extended to 25 October, but after that the Russian Jews would be treated in the same way as ordinary Englishmen in England or Russians in Russia. Readers of the letter were urged in the strongest terms, 'in honour and gratitude' not to hold back. But hold back they did. By 25 October, a bare 632 men had attested, and only 74 had enlisted for immediate service. The Jewish War Services Committee declared the voluntary scheme a failure.

Rationalising that the idea of voluntary service was anyway foreign to the Russians, who were accustomed to compulsion, and in a final bid to extract some measure of success from its efforts, the Committee suggested asking the Russian government to appeal to all Russian subjects resident in the United Kingdom to offer their services to the British Army under the same terms as British subjects. Most patriotic Russians had gone home when war broke out, leaving their revolutionary brethren behind – not a promising group for mobilisation in 1916.

2 The Russian Background

Immigrants do not change their social attitudes and behaviour overnight, even when they are strongly motivated to integrate into their newly adopted society, so that the resistance shown by recent Russian-Jewish refugees to the idea of military service to a large extent reflected the norms of their previous existence. Not that military service was the only determining factor in Russian-Jewish attitudes.

The Tsarist regime, from the latter part of the nineteenth century to the end of its existence in 1917, almost entirely excluded its five million or so Jewish subjects even from those plans for political reform that it did *not* implement, let alone those it did. The term 'alien' was applied to Jews. The English word 'alien' is translated into Russian variously as 'foreign' or 'foreigner', but rarely as '*inorodets*', which, conversely, is usually translated into English as 'alien', but rarely as 'foreigner'. Russian Jews were of course not 'foreigners' in Russia, but were Russian subjects. Lithuanians, Poles, Ukrainians and dozens of other groups were also Russian subjects, but only the Jews, along with the nomads of Siberia and the Muslims of Central Asia, were designated by the state that gave them their 'Russian' nationality as *inorodtsy*, literally, people of another breed.

This classification, while of some value to the nomads since it conferred a degree of autonomy, was for the Jews a heavy burden to bear, for it facilitated legislation to restrict the Jews within the Pale of Jewish Settlement, a narrow corridor corresponding roughly to Russia's European border, covering the Polish and Lithuanian provinces to the west and north-west, and the Ukrainian to the south. Some special categories of Jews were allowed to reside in Russia proper – very rich merchants who could qualify for membership of the First Guild by possession of at least 100,000 roubles of unentailed capital, their Jewish servants or employed artisans, university graduates, and former soldiers of Nicholas I's reign (1825–55). The rest had to survive as best they could within this Pale.

In the last two decades of the nineteenth century, when industry inside Russia 'proper' was being developed at 'American tempo', restrictions and discrimination against the Jews created such conditions in the Pale that by the end of the century it is estimated that almost 40 per cent of the total Jewish population of the Empire depended on charity provided by Jewish philanthropic institutions. In the decade leading up to the First World War, which included the revolutionary upheaval of 1905, widespread pogroms and mass emigration, those dependent on charity rose to 45 per cent. If we add to this the fact that, while many Jews in small hamlets engaged in agrarian occupations, the greater part of the Jews in the Russian Empire lived in townlets (*shtetls*), towns and cities, the picture is one of stark urban poverty endured by an entire national-religious, or ethnic, group, which had at the same time to endure the simmering and occasionally violent hostility of the other ethnic groups among whom they were compelled to dwell.

Jewish poverty was a distillation of European poverty. Industrialisation and the breakdown of the old order throughout Western and Central Europe had generated waves of emigration – from Germany, Italy, Britain, Ireland, Scandinavia and so on – which in turn created the rapid growth and variety of the population of the United States. In Russia, rapid industrialisation produced conditions of the utmost urban squalor and rural misery for masses of the population, including the majority of the Jews.

The restriction on movement suffered by the Russian Jews was mirrored to some extent by restraints endured by the Russians themselves. The peasants, and even more so the factory workers who were growing rapidly in number but who were mostly still legally classified as peasants, were watched by the police as potential sources of disorder and recruits for the illegal trade unions and revolutionary movement. They were not permitted to move around the country at will or without police permits. Great numbers of former peasants who were now factory workers were still legally inscribed in their village communities, through which they discharged their obligations to the state for taxation and military service, and this effectively put a brake on their mobility, to say nothing of their economic opportunities.

Despite these obstacles, from the reign of Alexander III (1881–94) onwards, industrialisation and economic modernisation was the policy to which the government was committed and from which it hoped to achieve economic strength and political stability. For this reason, administrative restraint and surveillance were more stringently exercised over workers inside the factories and factory-barracks where many were housed, than over the peasants in the villages. Yet paradoxically this was a time of physical mobility, as peasants and workers sought work wherever it was promised. The results speak for themselves: in the forty years since the emancipation of the serfs in 1861, the factory-worker population grew from one million to over eighteen million in 1900.*

Whatever the precise figure, it represents the rapid growth of Russian industrial investment and diversification and is evidence that official worries about political instability were outweighed by official calculation of the political benefit to be gained from economic strength. The fact that both these calculations would turn out to be wrong had more to do with the effects of the First World War than the social tensions created by tsarist economic policy.

The rise of industry in Russia was bound to cause an effect in the Pale. At the turn of the century, despite the restrictions, Jewish workers were moving to the new industrial areas of southern Russia and, in step with Russian development, their numbers there doubled. But nearly 80 per cent of the Russian-Jewish population in employment were either small traders (31 per cent), or artisans (36 per cent), of the latter nearly half worked in tailoring or similar trades, nearly 10 per cent were either manual labourers or domestics, and the rest were distributed in small percentages among the professions, in agriculture and the army.

The Jewish population was nowhere totally isolated from the other national groups, and in many *shtetls* they even outnumbered the Christian portion altogether. Often, the number of tailors and bootmakers would far exceed the local demand for their work. This drove them into making deals with bigger manufacturers from the towns, who would bring them materials, cloth and leather and credit at extortionate rates. While this arrangement might extricate a craftsman from a temporary crisis, it was only a short time before he felt himself imprisoned in debt and wage slavery. The Jewish Pale in this respect foreshadowed the sweatshops of the West which awaited so many at the end of their long journeys of emigration.

---

* Official statistics, which covered only enterprises employing at least twenty workers, gave a figure of three million. But by adding railway, dock, transportation and timber workers, as well as post and telegraph employees, and the vast number of artisans who fell outside the Ministry of Finance's remit, the total is more than eighteen million.

The picture of Russian-Jewish life was not all black – rather a range of greys with the occasional total eclipse and the equally rare ray of sunshine. One such ray had come with the accession of Alexander II in 1855, the 'Tsar Liberator' under whose auspices the serfs were emancipated, the legal system reformed, the universities and high schools expanded, and liberal-oriented local government institutions – *zemstvos* – created, and certain restraints lifted from the Jews, though not the injunction to remain within the Pale. Jews were admitted to Russian schools at all levels, as well as to universities, and as they struggled free of the religious restraints of their communities, young Jews found a congenial habitat in the Russian educational system. As they eagerly imbibed the new knowledge and culture, a new Russian-speaking, free-thinking Jewish intelligentsia was created.

Alexander's reforms also stimulated a more radical appetite for change among a large part of the educated Russian young, who preached that only a fundamental social revolution would satisfy the people's need for social justice, and the use of terrorism against the regime as an efficient means, with nothing less than the assassination of the 'Tsar Liberator' himself as the ultimate target. This aim was finally achieved on 1/13 March 1881.* The effect of the Tsar's murder was to bring an abrupt and total eclipse of reform and, far from a popular rising, only the passive silence of the masses. The immediate reaction of the new tsar, Alexander III, and those who advised him, was to throw the whole of the liberalising apparatus – the universities and *zemstvos*, in particular – into reverse.

Among the chief victims were the Jews. They were identified with the idea of change, especially change inspired by imported foreign notions, such as Marxism, and they were lumped together with the whole opposition movement whose extremist wing had been responsible for the murder of the tsar. Traditional Russian anti-Semitism exploded in a powerful surge of anti-liberalism, identifying those who wanted to modernise Russia with alien forces which wanted first to destroy Holy Russia. The Jews clearly fitted the bill as 'alien-minded': since most of them lived in abject poverty they

---

* Until February 1918, the Russian calendar lagged behind the Western (New Style) calendar by twelve days in the nineteenth century and thirteen days in the twentieth, thus 1 March 1881 (Old Style) was 13 March (New Style). New Style will generally be observed here, but to avoid ambiguity *both* styles may occasionally be indicated.

must have little love for Russia, and their alienation was being expressed by their Russian-educated elite in the form of violent revolutionary activity. The analysis, though grossly over-simplified, was certainly effective as nationalist propaganda, and it was not altogether off the mark, either.

Now all but shut out of Russian universities by a *numerus clausus*, or quota, of 10 per cent of the student body within the Pale and 5 per cent outside, and 3 per cent in Moscow and St Petersburg, and subjected to the severest tests for entry into high schools, where the quota was 5 per cent, young Jews began to seek education and professional qualifications in West European universities. Precisely at this time, young Russians were finding themselves similarly excluded, as growing numbers of student protesters were expelled from their studies and either sent into exile in Siberia or forced into the army or driven abroad. They grew to substantial numbers as the regime of Alexander III, and even more so that of his successor, Nicholas II, pressed harder and more efficiently on the rising revolutionary, trade union and liberal reform movements at the turn of the century.

However innocent or career-oriented young Jews may have been when setting out for the West, it would only be a short time before they were exposed to the revolutionary circles that sprang up around their universities in Zurich, Paris, Berlin, and changed from merely disaffected youth into organised oppositionists against the regime that had dashed their hopes. They began to fulfil the fears of the Russian secret police and to flood the ranks of the older, established Russian revolutionary groups abroad. In a short time they would begin to diversify into more ethnically based organisations, especially the Jewish socialist Bund and the Zionist movement, but in global terms they represented a scaled-down reflection of the deepening social and political crisis in Russia. And in just as short a time, they played a part in attempts that were being made by the Jewish workers inside Russia to organise their own way out of their misery, forming a labour movement that educated its members, and producing a political programme that embodied their emancipation as Jews and their responsibilities as workers and as part of an international brotherhood.

Such opportunities as there were for involvement in the political life of the country, the Jews gladly took. During the relatively good times of Alexander II Jews had become lawyers, doctors and teachers, and had formed a natural attachment to the movement for constitutional reform that had been instrumental in bringing local self-government into being from 1864. Up until 1890 Jews took an active part, as voters and members of these *zemstvo* boards, even though these did not exist in all the provinces of the Pale. As the Russian-Jewish Encyclopedia comments, 'evidently Russian society took no exception to this'. But in the atmosphere of growing Russian nationalism and its companion, anti-Semitism, a new edict of 1890 excluded Jews from local government in all its forms, 'pending a review of the regulations on the Jews'. This referred to the 'Temporary Regulations' of 1882 which had been the government's response to the wave of pogroms that followed the murder of Alexander II. Although called 'temporary', these arrangements would survive the upheaval of 1905 and the establishment of the Russian pseudo-parliament, the State Duma, and, apart from an adjustment during the First World War, were only swept away together with tsarism itself in the February Revolution of 1917.

The State Duma which came into its brief and troubled existence in 1906 was meant to be composed of all the nationalities of the Empire, and to establish the principle of their equality. Caught at a weak moment by defeat in the war with Japan and the universal demand for political reform, the tsarist regime for once did not exclude the Jews. They were permitted in theory to take part in the elections to the Duma on the same indirect suffrage as everyone else. And indeed the Jews expected to gain much from this new institution. But Russia's humiliating defeat at the hands of the Japanese in Manchuria, plus the double blows of having to concede democratic reforms and accept large loans from Jewish banks in Western Europe, had put both the government and conservative society into a deeply defensive mood. Counter-revolutionary bodies of vigilantes, so-called Black Hundreds – groups best described as proto-fascist – were organised, and with the help of the police set about 'discouraging' the Jews from taking part in the Duma elections. If anything, this only acted as an incentive to give even greater support to the party which most vigorously advocated equal rights, the liberal Constitutional Democrats, or Kadets. Twelve Jewish deputies were elected to the First Duma – ten Kadets and two Socialist Revolutionaries. Two of the Kadets would be murdered within a year. In common with the Bolsheviks and Mensheviks and the rest of the Russian Social Democratic Workers Party, the Jewish

Bund boycotted the Duma as a sham that would only serve to distract the workers from their revolutionary tasks.

Early in the short life of the First Duma – it was dissolved as unworkable after only 73 days – the Kadets raised the question of civil equality for all citizens, a matter of special urgency for the Jews who were at that moment suffering the worst pogroms seen in Russia since the seventeenth century. But the Duma was still too feverish from the effects of 1905 to function in the moderate and 'responsible' way the government had hoped for, and the legislation on civil equality remained only a dream until after the fall of the monarchy, when the liberal Provisional government introduced it as one of its first measures.

Elections to the Second Duma of early 1907 were even more enthusiastically supported by the Jews and now the slogan of 'full equality' was on all their banners. The Black Hundreds worked all the harder. In southern Russia among the Ukrainians, and in the Polish and Baltic provinces, the Russian Orthodox and Roman Catholic clergy warned their peasant flocks of dire spiritual punishment if they voted for the 'godless' liberals. Right-wing party candidates declared that 'a vote for the liberals was a vote for the Jews', and that a Jewish victory would be bought at the peasants' cost. This time the campaign was more effective. The number of Jewish deputies elected fell from twelve to four, three Kadets and one Social Democrat, (the latter party, having seen the publicity gained by the Kadets in action, now decided that the Duma might be useful as a 'soapbox' for their own propaganda). But this was also in part the result of new regulations which restricted both the categories and numbers of Jewish voters. Yet despite the government's efforts to weight the electoral system against the left-wing and progressive parties, the Second Duma turned out to be so sharply combative and oppositional in character, thanks mainly to the presence of the socialists, that it too was dissolved after a brief life of under four months, and it produced nothing of value to any class of the population.

In spite of a new electoral law of 3/16 June 1907, passed while the Duma was suspended and designed to cut the Jews and their liberal friends down to size in the Third Duma, the Jews once again returned to the ballot box in the face of open hostility from the police and local population. With the Kadets much reduced and the Jewish deputies down to two, the new assembly was dominated by a reactionary, chauvinistic claque which the government hoped would give its legislation the spurious respectability of a parliamentary veneer. While the liberals tried in vain to raise the 'Jewish Question' under the guise of general issues of civil rights, the Right indulged in mud-slinging, and the Centre, or moderate conservative parties, tried to advance their own (largely economic) goals by avoiding such 'thorny issues'.

As a result, the legislative projects that were presented to the Duma only added to the burden of disabilities already being borne by the Jews. Restrictions, as the Jewish Encyclopedia put it, 'ran like a red thread through all the proposed legislation brought into the Duma. Whether the debate was on a new institute of statistics, the Don Polytechnic, women's teacher training schools, elementary schools, the Vilna Medical Auxiliary School, or categories for exemption from taxation, special restrictions were included for the Jews.'

One of the parties to emerge from the 1905 Revolution was the Union of 17 October, or the Octobrists, so named because they accepted Nicholas II's October 1905 Manifesto as a basis for the peaceful political reconstruction of Russia. As a party it was committed to representative government and reform and, although its members were a coalition that stretched to Russian nationalists on the Right, its leader, Alexander Guchkov, was dedicated to the goal of implementing the rule of law for the first time in Russia. In the face of the most hostile contempt of the Tsar and the Tsarina towards him, Guchkov would in due course emerge as one of the government's most vigorous critics; as a champion of the voluntary bodies that would support the war effort after 1914; as one of the two emissaries from the Duma who in March 1917 would demand the Tsar's abdication; and he would become the first Minister of War in the Provisional government. Alexander Guchkov in short was unequivocally an opposition politician. Yet in 1910 it was Guchkov who proposed that Jewish doctors henceforth be prohibited from entering the army medical service, and it was from the Octobrists that the even more radical – and unsuccessful – proposal came that Jews be excluded from the army altogether, and that a special tax be levied on them in lieu of military service. Clearly, both the Russian government and the conservative elements of opposition were united in pursuing policies that were good for the 'responsible elements' of society, namely the wealthy property-owners, and could at the same time be perceived as good for the 'true Russian people'; policies intended to show that the regime was not going soft on the Jews and their liberal friends.

Ever susceptible to the idea that their lives were being manipulated by some conspiracy or other, Russian anti-Semites were fertile soil for the *Protocols of the Elders of Zion*, a document concocted by the Russian secret police in 1897 and published in 1903 on the eve of the Kishinev (today's Chisinau) pogrom and again in 1905, and purporting to prove that, through the Jewish-owned banks of Western Europe, the Jews were plotting to take over the world. It was exposed by *The Times* as a forgery in 1920, and will resurface here later.

There were Jewish bankers and magnates in Russia, but they were neither numerous nor prominent in public life, they did not hold the same sort of dominant positions as their counterparts in Hamburg or Paris, whose great banks, as it happens, actually came to the rescue of the Russian state in the costly reckoning of the war with Japan. Nor did they have the importance of those in the City of London, whose links with the British establishment demonstrated their integration into the host society, not its opposite. In any case, the money market did not play the same central role in Russian economic life as it did in the West: in Russia the state itself was capitalism's chief banker and chief customer. The overwhelming majority of Russian Jews were in fact crushed by poverty, and after 1905 nearly half were still living on charity. Economically, the Jews, rich and poor alike, were a marginal group in Russia, although neither their marginality nor their general lack of wealth protected them from the accusation that they were exploiting the Russian people. They were highly visible in petty trade and commerce and the drinking houses of the provinces of the Pale, and were therefore a convenient target during hard times.

While most of the population of the cities of the Pale were ethnic Russians – and many Jews – the non-Jewish population of the Pale consisted substantially of Ukrainians, Belorussians, Poles, Romanians, Estonians, Latvians and Lithuanians. Of these only the Ukrainians and Belorussians were of the Russian Orthodox faith, although part of the Ukrainian population, the so-called Uniates, also recognised the Pope in Rome. The others were either Roman Catholic or Lutheran. No less important than their religious affiliations was their shared hostility to the Russian Imperial government which oppressed them, robbed them of their national heritage and, especially in its last years, was exerting a heavy-handed policy of russification which was supposed to stifle their nationalism but of course achieved the opposite. Paradoxically, the russification policy weighed least of all on the Jews who, if anything, felt they were being prevented from entering into Russian life and culture.

With the rise of nationalism and national liberation movements in Europe, especially in the multinational Austro-Hungarian Empire, the Russian government was bound to view its national minorities, amounting to more than half the total population, with some caution. Plainly, if all the non-Russian nationalities were to unite – an impossible fantasy – the regime's stability would be put under extreme stress. But even within themselves the national minorities did not all possess the features of unitary nations. The idea of nationhood and a national culture, though strong among some minorities, in others was something that had to be created in the nineteenth century by a small (and invariably russified) intelligentsia. The minority populations of western and southern Russia were mostly poor peasants whose ethnic solidarity emerged most often only when they vented their frustrations on the most convenient 'alien' element to hand, namely the Jews.

Anti-Semitism, whipped up among the non-Russians by officially inspired Russian groups, has commonly been interpreted as the safety valve used by the tsarist regime to let off steam that might otherwise explode in the face of the administration. To this extent, it showed that the regime was sensitive to potential sources of ethnic unrest. And indeed by the turn of the century, many of the national minorities, including the Jews, had created their own political parties and revolutionary organisations. They had launched themselves on the path of national liberation, or else had attached themselves to the mainstream Russian revolutionary organisations, particularly the Marxist Social Democrats. The Jews were regarded by the regime as a special danger in this regard, since they were not concentrated in a particular territory, but were scattered among the Russian revolutionary intelligentsia in general. And since they were thought of as associated with 'internationalism', via world Jewry, their revolutionary doctrines were likely to be universal in appeal and less limited to one national goal. The Jews, in other words, were seen as a uniquely seditious element.

Another and more widespread aspect of Russian anti-Semitism was its religious component. The fact that many Orthodox Russian clergy openly preached sermons against the 'Jewish peril' and were involved in right-wing manipulation of the elections to the Duma shows the natural link between primitive 'Christian' folklore and the accusation of Christ-killing levelled against the Jewish people as a whole. Powers of witchcraft and black magic were ascribed to the Jews in much of peasant lore, in Russia as elsewhere in Europe. In Russia the accusations reached their climax in the notorious Beilis Affair of 1911–13, when a Jew, Mendel Beilis, was charged with the ritual murder of a Christian boy, whose blood, it was alleged, was to be used in the ritual baking of unleavened bread for the Passover meal. This contorted association of ideas, combining the Jewish murder of a Christian and a perverted rehearsal of Christ's narrative on the bread and wine at the Last Supper (arguably his last Passover meal), would have a powerful effect on the mind of a superstitious peasant. Civilised society in Russia and the rest of the world was scandalised by the Beilis affair and by the depths to which the tsarist regime had sunk in its efforts to maintain the unity of the Russian nation. As for Beilis, he was acquitted and ended up as an insurance agent in the USA.

Given that Jewish identity in Russia was legally determined as attachment to Judaism, and not to a national group, it followed that for legal purposes conversion to Orthodox Christianity should have brought full equality. Conversion was indeed chiefly motivated by such considerations. In the course of the nineteenth century, twice as many Russian Jews converted to Russian Orthodoxy as had Jews in Austria-Hungary, who provided the most converts in Western Europe, including missionary-minded Britain. Before 1905 in Russia mixed marriages were permitted on condition that the Jewish partner convert and that he or she convert only to Russian Orthodoxy; after 1905 Jews could intermarry, but only with Protestants. But the actual figures – only 84,000 in the whole of the nineteenth century – suggest that conversion was not an important feature of Jewish life in Russia, or elsewhere for that matter. Nor did the regime engage in energetic proselytising among the Jews.

The anti-Semitic policies of late tsarism were the product of multiple, often contradictory elements: religious anti-Judaism, racial prejudice, national hostility, conservative hatred of foreign influences, the need for a scapegoat at a time when Russian institutions and values were under siege, exploitation of popular prejudices in order to foster national unity. In short, anti-Semitism was an institutional fact of life in Russia and formed the framework within which the Jews were joining the exodus from Europe to the New World and other points en route.

The legal discrimination might be thought to have affected mainly the better-off or educated sections of the Russian-Jewish population, but inevitably, in a generally hostile environment, the legal disabilities that hampered the better-off would in turn have damaging effects on the poorer classes. If a Jewish manufacturer or merchant was being squeezed by the corrupt local authorities and made to pay dearly for their tolerance, then he was bound to shift this pressure to his labour force. The 'sweatshops' of Whitechapel in London, Belleville in Paris and the Lower East Side in New York had their origins in the Pale. In an effort to understand the great urge to emigrate from Russia – and bearing in mind that most emigrants had not had direct experience of the pogroms – it is reasonable to suggest that their main reason for leaving was to improve their lives. The economic motive is reinforced by the fact that thousands of non-Jewish Russian subjects were emigrating at the same time, mainly to the USA and Canada, though many of them did not intend to stay away any longer than it took to make some money and return home.

It was argued, usually by Marxist revolutionaries, Jewish and non-Jewish alike, that all the working masses in the end were suffering from the same exploitation, whether they were of this nationality or that. The promise of the socialist revolution was that it would sweep away all forms of oppression, economic and political, national and ethnic. The Jews would be emancipated like everyone else. In this internationalist doctrine it was inconceivable that the working class of one nation could ever oppress the working class of another. The Jewish workers and their families who were most affected by the atmosphere of pogroms, and who were aware that the pogromists were poor workers like themselves, were neither convinced by this promise, nor were they content to sit and wait for the revolution. What they did believe was that Jews could live like other people in the West, and that in Russia they were at best second-class citizens. Thus, when the Russian Jews in Britain faced the question of military service, their champions could defend them as refugees from tsarist oppression and religious persecution.

The definition of their status changed together with the shifts of the Russian Revolution and the last stages of the war on the Eastern Front. But when the question of military service for these 'friendly aliens' in Britain was first raised, they were represented as political and not economic refugees. Immigrants could not fairly be said to be escaping from their homeland: they were rather coming in search of a better life; refugees – asylum-seekers, in modern parlance – had to be escaping from some defined threat, their choice of refuge being determined only by the readiness of another country to accept them. Active legislation against the Jews continued to be passed in Russia, even after the events of 1905 had demonstrated to an alarmed administration that political and civil rights were desired by the whole of society. (In Britain, the flood of refugees from Russia prompted parliament to pass the country's first Aliens Act in 1905.) And having noted the activities of the Black Hundreds and the wave of pogroms that swept parts of the Pale, and the show trial of Beilis, it would be fair to say that, even if the Jews were not driven out of Russia, but chose to go, and even if the great majority still remained there, those who did emigrate saw themselves as both refugees and immigrants.

Russia was anything but a free country; the workers and peasants lived in the most miserable conditions under the baleful eye of the police and the land captains, who acted as rural watchdogs; if an educated person expressed an interest in politics and concern for the future of the country by joining a banned organisation – which most were – they were inviting ruin for themselves, or worse. Given that within this setting of rightlessness the Jews were consistently singled out for still fewer rights, it is not surprising that large sections of the Jewish population were simply alienated. The fact that so many Jews identified with the future of the country was as much evidence of their faith in the new society that must emerge from The Revolution, as their attachment to Russian culture.

With all their disabilities – educational, legal and economic – the Jews were nevertheless treated as equals when it came to the question of military service. In this respect they differed from their co-aliens, the Muslims of Central Asia and the nomads of Siberia. The principle of commonality, which was established in 1874 in order to create a 'nation in arms' based on universal conscription, was soon eroded as far as the Jews were concerned. While liability to conscription was universal, recruitment itself was carried out by lottery, as the number of available men of military age always far exceeded the 800,000 required for the standing peacetime army, as well as the 500,000 kept in reserve. Since the Russian population was growing at an explosive rate at the end of the nineteenth century, the proportion of men recruited to those left out was constantly shrinking. Exemption and deferment on educational grounds were fairly freely allowed: in general, university students could defer up to the age of 27 or 28 (probably an explanation of the phenomenon of the 'eternal student' to be found around Russian universities). Family circumstances were also taken into account when ballot results were examined, but other than physical fitness it was the conditions of peasant life that mostly dictated the reasons for exemption.

If a Russian Christian was entitled to exemption, the rule was that he should be replaced by another Christian, or another member of his family. If it was found that the exempted man was a converted Jew, then his place could only be taken by a Jew. The medical fitness and physical size of Jewish recruits was permitted to be inferior to what was required for Russians. Deferment for a Jew, granted by the recruitment authorities for whatever reason, could be rescinded without notice and immediate call-up ordered. Rewards for the capture of Jews who tried to evade call-up were paid from a special budget, according to a scale set by the Ministry of the Interior. Further rules were designed to ensure that, on completion of military service, a Jew, wherever he might have served, should return to his original place of residence in the Pale: the cover of his discharge book was stamped, 'Not a Residence Permit.'

Perhaps the most onerous rule was the 300 roubles fine which the family faced when a man failed to show up when called. He could be in hospital and even be in possession of a police certificate to prove it, yet his failure to appear at the call-up gave the self-same police the excuse to exact the fine. As the average *annual* wage of a skilled artisan in 1900 was 300–400 roubles, and that of young men approaching military age usually less, the effect of a 300-rouble fine can easily be imagined, and this, as much as anything, was a prime cause for the desperate steps Jews took to escape both the hazards of conscription and the consequences of failure to turn up.

Its anti-Semitic prejudices apart, the government applied these severe sanctions against the Jews because it was convinced that the Jews consistently failed to provide their full quota of recruits. But the figures on which the authorities based their calculations were extremely unreliable. The mechanism of registration and control in Russia was more reminiscent of early nineteenth-century bureaucracy than that of a twentieth-century state that was pursuing a policy of modernisation. Registration in Russia was haphazard, as the papers of many a Russian-Jewish family would show. The most common confusion was caused by the garbling of names in their transcription from spoken Yiddish to written Russian. Had Jews been allowed to take Russian names, life might have been easier. But the only concession was the right to adapt one's Hebrew-Yiddish name to its nearest-sounding Russian diminutive. Hence, Yasha and Masha and Misha and Grisha, all perfectly good *Russian* diminutives of Yakob, Maria, Mikhail and Grigory, and corresponding to Yaacov, Miriam, Michal and Gershon in Hebrew. Russian clerks, at the level encountered by poor, illiterate Jews, were often simply incapable of rendering a reliable transcription. Anecdotes and jokes about the confusion over their 'strange names' when Jews reached Ellis Island or London usually derived from their experience at the hands of non-Jewish officials.

Another flaw in the official statistics derived from the fact that, if a Jew died in a different place from that in which he was registered as liable for military service, his death would often not be noted in the proper place and his failure to report for duty would show up as a shortfall in the figures. Given the effects of mass emigration in the years before the First World War, much of it illegal, and bearing in mind that on average 60 per cent of emigrants were men, and about 70 per cent of them were aged between 14 and 44, it is easy to see that the list of phantoms the Russian Army expected to become conscripts was growing steadily, along with official exasperation.

The result of these deficiencies was that the government believed the Jews were under-represented in the army, and this offended its sense of the duties of the citizenry, even the second-class citizenry. In fact, according to a statistical analysis of the official evidence, the government's impression was an illusion. In statistical terms, throughout the period from the 1880s to the eve of the First World War, the Jews consistently provided a disproportionately *larger* number of recruits than any other national, ethnic or religious group. This situation arose, not from greater patriotism or willingness, but simply from the ineptness of the system.

Out of roughly 1,000,000 Christians liable for conscription each year, 300,000 or 30 per cent were actually recruited. Between 1880 and 1909, 425,000 Jews performed military service, that is, 33 per cent or 20,000 of the roughly 60,000 liable annually. In 1897 the Jews constituted 4.13 per cent of the overall population and 5.2 per cent of the Russian Army. It is doubtful whether the Jewish communities were fully aware of this over-representation, and it certainly went unnoticed, or unremarked, by the military authorities.

In the years 1900 to 1914, then, about 300,000 Jews had experience of the Russian Army. While many of them were put to work as army tailors – a trade which occupied as many as 12 per cent of all enlisted men – most would have been trained as ordinary soldiers and, of the 80,000 active during the Russo-Japanese War, many fought as gunners and infantrymen, sappers and cavalrymen, as they would again during the First World War. Numerous accounts appeared in 1904 and 1905, even in the anti-Semitic press, of the bravery and reliability of the Jewish troops fighting in Manchuria. Russian officers testified to cases of exemplary and inspiring conduct by Jews when Christian troops needed morale-boosting. Many Jews were awarded high decorations for bravery, some more than once. Probably it was this public notice of the Jewish contribution that prompted the Tsar, when announcing the birth of his son and heir in 1904, to grant the right of free settlement anywhere in the Empire to Jewish soldiers who had served with distinction. In practice, this privilege was granted only rarely, and there were many press reports of Jewish ex-soldiers applying for it in vain. My father's army discharge book, showing an unblemished war record, was of no use as a residence permit, but it did serve as an internal passport and was used for police stamps allowing him to travel to a particular destination within the Pale for a specified length of time.

Perhaps Russia's ignominious defeat in the war against Japan cancelled out any benefit to the Jews that might have been gained by the gallantry of Jewish soldiers, but an army discharge book was nevertheless a thing of value, the most concrete rebuttal to anti-Semitic jibes about the Jews being unwilling to serve in the army. (My father was conscripted into the Russian Army in 1902 and discharged at the end of 1905, having taken part in the Manchurian campaign. His discharge book shows his age, place of birth, religion, marital status (single), length of service and under 'special features of his service' it also states that he 'served in campaigns against the Japanese, took part in battles in 1904–5'.) Such a document would have been carried with pride, and also with some confidence that it might offset the rudeness and bloody-mindedness encountered by Jews – and most other members of the lower orders – when they needed the customary 'scrap of paper' for some official purpose. Those with the foresight to hang onto their discharge book would find it of inestimable value, sometimes as a matter of life and death, during the chaos that reigned in Russia in the Revolution and Civil War to come.

Army service in Russia was tough. The harsh discipline thought necessary to instil orderliness into the ignorant peasants was extended to recruits of all classes, nationalities and religions. Jewish religious services were generally permitted, but in the brutal climate of the ranks Jewish conscripts suffered mockery and often physical abuse for their un-Christian way of prayer. The army made no allowance for Jewish soldiers hoping to maintain a kosher diet, and unless a rabbi issued a dispensation it was a case of 'eat or starve', and few chose to starve. The proximity of a local Jewish community, with its common practice of feeding the needy, was the only partial and temporary solution.

Every Jewish recruit would have felt the free-floating anti-Semitism, yet the experience of military service, particularly if it included active war service, no doubt instilled in many a Jewish soldier a measure of toughness and self-reliance that would stand him in good stead in unpromising circumstances later. Despite this 'positive' side of military service, countless Jews of military age made every effort to evade conscription, and emigration was the main route by which they succeeded. The majority of emigrants were artisans – tailors, shoemakers, cabinet-makers, watchmakers, etc. – men whose skills were in demand in Britain and America. Since no regular system of emigration existed in Russia, and would-be emigrants tended to stumble over bureaucratic trip-wires the moment they first applied for a passport, an illegal exodus soon came into being. It was operated by unscrupulous shipping agents seeking skilled workers for firms in Whitechapel, Manchester, Glasgow or Chicago and New York. This smuggling of human contraband offered rich pickings for crooks and confidence-men, and stories of deceit and tragedy abound.

Not that things were much better for legal emigrants. The Russian border gendarmes who processed emigrants made it their 'duty' to isolate the Jews from the local populace 'in order to reduce the risk of spreading infectious diseases', their true purpose being simply to provide a captive market for the German shipping companies which paid them. Parties of emigrants were kept in filthy barracks, which they could leave only with a permit from the stationmaster; they had to buy their food from stalls which were licensed by the same stationmaster, and buy their boat tickets at the border post under duress and with no choice and less idea of what they were in for or even where they might end up. A ticket bought for New York might easily turn out to have been paid for only as far as London or Newcastle.

The opportunities for graft, in both the legal and illegal systems, were simply legion. Having crossed into Prussia, emigrants were forced to surrender their roubles for German money at a poor rate; they were made to go through a bath and disinfection, for which they had to pay, and they were under constant threat of summary return to Russia in case they protested against the harsh treatment. On the Austrian border in Galicia, where there were no control posts, emigrants were entirely in the hands of agents and smugglers. Little glory is reflected on some Jewish agencies, as most of the crooked agents were themselves Jews, as were most of the owners of the sweatshops waiting for the hopeful new immigrants.

With an annual emigration rate of about 200,000 by 1905, of which the greater part was no longer composed of Jews but included many Poles and Baltic peoples, the Russian government was finally moved to give some thought to establishing a proper procedure. But up until 1914 no legislation was passed to regulate emigration, and would-be emigrants, of all ethnic origins, still had to go through the costly hoops of bureaucracy and corruption as before. For the Jews, there were at least a number of bureaux set up by the Jewish Colonisation Association in the main Russian centres of Jewish population, and through these it was possible for legal emigrants to minimise the red tape and ruinous 'tariffs'.

A counterpoint to this picture of gloom and escape was the almost equally remarkable phenomenon of Jewish assimilation of Russian culture and customs. Jewish history, the languages spoken throughout the Diaspora, dress, folklore and outlook, all combine to show that the Jews of the Diaspora were assimilationists par excellence. Wherever they settled they acquired colouring from their new habitat, regardless of how persistently they may also have clung to the values which they regarded as transcendent and inalienable from their sense of being Jewish. By means of language, outer trappings and social and economic intercourse, the Jews maintained creative relationships with both the host nations and their own communities.

But they were themselves powerfully influenced in turn through those same channels. In the Russia of the second half of the nineteenth century the influence of social and economic change was strong enough to break down the traditional values of Jewish society, as it was doing to large sections of Russian society. Assimilation was the vehicle which carried many Jews out of the ghetto, in spirit if not always physically. Assimilation expressed itself in many ways – Jews began to become lawyers and doctors, artists and musicians – but perhaps one of the most striking new directions was in political life. Resistant to religious conversion and mostly cut off from the economic vitality of Russia proper, in the history of the Russian revolutionary and labour movements, the Jewish organisations which were created in the late nineteenth and early twentieth centuries occupied a significant position.

Revolutionary organisations proliferated in Russia at a rate that overstretched the resources of the secret police. The creation of cells, underground networks for spreading revolutionary propaganda, illegal printing presses, the smuggling of banned literature from abroad, and above all the formation of political parties, produced an atmosphere of impending change that was reflected in the Jewish world, illustrating the resonance that existed between the lives of the Jews and the society around them. And as Jews slackened their hold on their traditions, it was the ways of the surrounding society that replaced them. Even Jewish intellectuals who turned to Zionism, when it arrived at the end of the century, were mostly assimilated, Russian-speaking and Russian-educated.

The Jewish working classes of Eastern Europe were exposed to the ideas of the labour movement as soon as it came into being. The artisans of the Pale were converting their mutual aid societies – dating back to the 1840s – into strike funds and trade unions as early as the 1880s. Illiterate and impoverished as they were, they were nevertheless receptive to simplified Marxist teaching on economic exploitation and the lack of political rights to a degree that was the envy of Russian revolutionaries who were trying, and mostly failing, to awaken the Russian worker and peasant – the two were not always distinguishable – to these vital questions. The life of the emigrants in London and New York was marked by the central place occupied by their trade unions, and all this activity was brought out of the towns of the Pale by the same impoverished masses. By the same process of symbiosis as they acquired the Russian drive for organisation, the Jews also absorbed Russian attitudes to the army and the ever-present threat of compulsory service.

3 Russian Jews and the War

In terms of military service, with the exception of Britain, all the countries taking part in the First World War treated their Jews like the rest of their citizens, in principle if not always in practice. Jews formed significant minorities in all of the belligerent countries and, after April 1917 when the United States entered the war on the side of the Allies, there would also be a sizeable Jewish component on the other side of the Atlantic. The total number of men mobilised by all sides in the conflict has been estimated as 65 million, and the total number of Jews in all armies about 2.16 million, or 3.3 per cent. According to Abraham Druker's analysis of the Jewish contribution to all the belligerents, of the 42 million men mobilised by the Allies, Jews accounted for 1.06 million, or 2.5 per cent. Those in the Russian Army alone amounted to about 600,000 or 4.5 per cent. Of the 23 million men in the forces of the Central Powers (Germany and Austria-Hungary), Jews numbered just under half a million, or 2.17 per cent. The number of Jews killed in action, 171,000, represented 2.6 per cent of all losses.

But statistics played little part in forming public opinion and public policy when, despite the evidence, questions arose about the willingness or unwillingness of the Jews to carry their share of the burden of war. The issue was also complicated by the fact that, while citizens of Jewish origin were under an equal obligation, the distinction was often blurred between them and aliens who also happened to be Jews but who were not liable and who needed to be nudged into service beyond the normal duties of an alien.

The French, whose universal conscription came into operation at the beginning of the war, were the first to approach the issue of compulsory military service for friendly aliens, in particular how to deal with the Russian Jews who numbered about 100,000 in total, of whom about 20,000 were of military age. The French government wanted no repetition of the Dreyfus Affair which had raised the issue of Jewish loyalties, and decided the best course was to appoint an independent commission to examine the question. It was chaired by a state counsellor and included representatives of the Prefecture of the Police and Ministry of the Interior, two judges, and the eminent professor of sociology at the Sorbonne, David Emile Durkheim. Although a Jew by origin himself, Durkheim was highly assimilated and had shown no interest whatever in the 'Jewish Question', and was therefore assumed to be able to carry out the task with sympathy for the subjects and detached judgment on the state's behalf.

When Durkheim agreed to serve he began by carrying out a survey to determine the part the Russian Jews were already playing in the Allied war effort. He found that about 9,000, or slightly less than half the eligible number, had volunteered at the outbreak of war, and this led the commission unanimously to recommend that nothing more be done. The Durkheim report was submitted at the end of February 1916, the government accepted its conclusions, the commission was dissolved and the anti-Semites fell silent, coming back to life only when Herbert Samuel made his announcement in the British Parliament three months later.

Durkheim was now prompted to submit a further report with the aim of minimising the potential ill effects of British policy on French opinion. He reminded the government that the anti-Semitic agitation, boosted by jingoistic speeches in the Chamber of Deputies, had begun the previous summer and that the government had given in to right-wing pressure and set up the commission of inquiry which it hoped would prick the Russian-Jewish conscience. Despite the apparently mild nature of this measure, the Russian-Jewish community, 'always in a nervous state', had reacted badly, anticipating persecution. Many had emigrated to Spain and the United States, where they were greeted by pro-German elements who paraded them as living testimony to French anti-Semitism. Articles had appeared in the New York Yiddish press and letters were sent from New York urging the Jews of Paris to flee French persecution.

Durkheim pointed out that France's vital interests required careful management of American opinion – especially Jewish American opinion – which was sensitive to anything concerning Jews. For this reason, a Propaganda and Action Committee had been established to promote pro-Allied views among the Jews of neutral countries. This cause had been damaged by the government's proposed measures against the Russian-Jewish émigrés and Durkheim and his colleagues on the committee were now determined to stop the rot before it was too late.

The main objection to the British case was that it blatantly violated the right of asylum. The Russian Jews, whether in France or Britain, were political or religious refugees and were therefore unable to exercise a real choice between serving in the local army or returning to Russia, where the 'politicals' would face prison or exile, while those who were motivated by religious considerations would face renewed persecution. And, since political refugees would not have the right to serve in the Russian Army, it was immoral to press them to serve in France.* As for religious refugees, although they had that right, they knew from bitter experience what life held for them in Russia.

It was accepted that the émigrés owed something to the country that sheltered them, but it was argued that France had no right to demand that they repay her by military service. 'We do not ask it of Romanian Jewish immigrants. Why then should we do so of Russian Jews who have nothing to do with Russia any more? When refugees gather in a particular country, they are not citizens of that country. They do not have all the obligations because they do not have all the rights. Are we going to let the Germans and the pro-Germans champion the right of asylum and hold us and the English up to the neutrals as persecutors of the Jews?' The measures announced by the British government, Durkheim predicted, would expose the British to even harsher criticism. 'It will be said that the English have been more indulgent to themselves than to the wretched foreigners to whom they have given hospitality. It took them more than a year and a half to introduce conscription, a fact which alone showed that it was a controversial subject in England. And only two months later, they want to impose it on foreigners who are not British citizens.'

The French government's 'admonitions' had led to nothing, except Jewish emigration and fresh attacks from the anti-Semites. In the name of the Action Committee, Durkheim urged the British Home Secretary to declare publicly that the situation in England was different from that in France, since Russians in France had already volunteered in large numbers, which was why the French government had decided to go no further. His report ended: 'This

---

* Durkheim, it appears, was unaware that the Russian government for many years had been sending young revolutionaries into the army as an alternative to prison.

will prevent the French anti-Semites from exploiting the English example, and might minimise the damage.' When Lucien Wolf, as Secretary of the Foreign Conjoint Committee, went to Paris in the summer of 1916 to discuss the issue with leading Jewish figures, Durkheim told him the whole scheme had evaporated because 'the game was not worth the candle', and Wolf duly conveyed this to Herbert Samuel.

What of Russia's war effort? By the summer of 1917 she had mobilised 12 million men. Of these, 1.7 million were killed, 4.9 million were wounded, 2.5 million were either prisoners of war or missing in action, meaning that a staggering 76.31 per cent of the total mobilised were out of action. For Russians, the issue of military service arose in an entirely different social, political and historical context from that of Russia's allies. Military service, once the lot of the peasants, had been compulsory for all classes since the middle of the 1870s. Along with the falling proportion demanded of a fast-growing male population, the length of service in Alexander II's reformed army had been reduced from six to four and then, after the Russo-Japanese War, three years, with twelve years in the reserve. At the outbreak of war active service was raised again to four years and the age of liability dropped from 21 to 20. The only exempt groups were the clergy, the Finns, and certain tribes of the Caucasus, Siberia and Central Asia. These exceptions were insignificant when compared to the rest of the population of 175,000,000, and somewhat special when set against the great variety of minorities who were not exempt, such as the Ukrainians, Poles, Latvians and other Balts, and the Jews. Russian military service was, then, a universal obligation, operated universally, at least in principle.*

The introduction of universal conscription in the 1870s was aimed at raising the efficiency of the army by making it a truly national body – 'the nation in arms' – rather than one whose officer class was dominated by the nobility and therefore identified with the monarchy, while the grey mass of peasants dumbly bore the yoke of service. And yoke it was. Russian peasants regarded military service as a scourge, a penance for sins unknown, and above all as an assault on the economic life of the family and the community, since

---

* When the Muslims of Central Asia were threatened with conscription in the middle of 1916 they staged a mass uprising which in effect launched the national liberation movements of the empire's Asian territories, setting the scene for the eventual demarcation of the Central Asian Soviet republics in 1924.

it inevitably deprived them of their most vital source of labour. Since their emancipation in 1861, by the twentieth century the Russian peasants, taken as a whole, were overwhelmed by indebtedness, falling living standards, diminishing returns from the land and a growing sense of despair.

Nevertheless, the last years of the old regime were not a time of universal misery leading inexorably to the outburst of 1917. Many individual peasants had had the enterprise, ability and good luck to take advantage of the decline of the Russian landowning gentry which took place over the second half the nineteenth century, and to become landowners themselves. During the last fifteen years of the nineteenth century and right up to the outbreak of the First World War, Russian social and economic life saw rapid and positive changes. The agrarian reforms brought about by Prime Minister Peter Stolypin from 1906 to 1911, though ultimately unsuccessful, did have a beneficial effect on parts of the peasant economy. Also, masses of peasants and workers migrated to promising places throughout the empire, including Siberia. The establishment of great industrial complexes employing thousands of workers, as well as entirely new branches, such as oil, came into being, and in general great new wealth was created.

But nothing in Russia was unadulterated, every positive achievement brought negative effects. The vast numbers of urban poor and uprooted, disoriented industrial workers created chronic, seemingly incurable discontent. And the eternal peasant question would not go away. The peasants who remained tied to the land, if only by taxation, resisting the forces of development that drove millions into the cities, bitterly resented any time they had to spend away from their sacred soil. For most of them, their economy was so precarious that even their worker-cousins had to migrate seasonally in their millions from factories back to the villages to help with the harvest. Given the peasants' tenuous hold on their own economy, evading military service was widespread and often took extreme form. Conscripts went to the lengths of self-mutilation, shooting off the trigger-finger, or drinking a pint of vinegar before the medical examination to induce, so they believed, the visible symptoms of anaemia. Recruit assembly points were often the scene of drunken riots. For the great mass of recruits, uneducated and utterly apathetic, army service meant harsh discipline and, although they might be better fed than at home and might even learn some useful skills, such as basic literacy, they were plagued by a gnawing obsession to get back to the land. (In 1917 Lenin accelerated the mounting disintegration of the Russian Army by urging the peasants to leave the trenches, go home to their villages and seize the land for themselves.)

The peasants provided the bulk of Russia's conscript army, but Russia's urban population was increasing fast and her army therefore also reflected the growing complexity of society. Especially during the war, when the turnover of intakes was accelerated by Russia's huge losses, the mixed nature of the army was to prove one of the most powerful political elements in the revolutionary events of 1917. Articulate, better-educated and self-taught worker-soldiers in the ranks exercised considerable influence on their peasant-comrades, who only knew that they wanted to get out of the trenches and away from the senseless slaughter, but who needed credible leaders to voice their desires.

The ethnic composition of the army would also be instrumental in breaking up rather than holding the army together. In the anarchic conditions of 1917, soldiers belonging to minorities were quick to form 'national' regiments in order to achieve and defend the independence of their own people in the post-tsarist settlement, however it turned out. The Russian Army, in other words, was not an undifferentiated mass of peasants-in-uniform, but an army of the whole of Russian society, similar in its ethnic complexity to the army of the Austro-Hungarian Empire.*

Only ten years before the First World War, in its failed attempt to master Manchuria in the face of Japanese expansion, the Russian Empire had undergone its severest test since the Crimean War. In addition to the army's defeats, the main Russian battle fleet was sunk in the Sea of Japan in a single afternoon. The whole of Russian society had been in a state of ferment and revolt for the best part of a year, demanding political reform from the Tsar and threatening the regime as never before. The political trauma that shook the Russian government in 1905 had arisen directly from the distant and seemingly pointless war in Manchuria, and although turbulence in the armed forces was less than it might have been, universal conscription inevitably meant that the soldiers were affected by the mood of unrest

---

* The Austro-Hungarian Army also came apart along its ethnic seams in the last throes of the Central Powers' war effort.

in society at large. Soldiers, of course, were deterred from open revolt
by the knowledge that, as long as the line of command remained
intact, mutiny carried with it far heavier penalties than those inflicted
on civilians, except for acts of armed revolt.

In contrast to the Russo-Japanese War, the outbreak of the First
World War was greeted in Russia by an outburst of patriotic fervour.
Professor Bernard Pares, one of the earliest British academic specialists on Russia and the official British observer with the Russian
Army in the field, recorded in his diary that in the Duma every
section of political opinion and every race in the Russian Empire
declared its loyalty and devotion, and he noted that 'no speeches left
a greater impression than those of the Lithuanians and of the Jews'.
For the public and the Duma itself these speeches were a revelation.
'The war thus had a national character ... and was a great act in the
national life of Russia.'

At this relatively early stage in the war, Pares was writing his
diary for British public opinion, and was keen to encourage enthusiasm for the Russian war effort. Although in the spring of 1917 he
was as close to the Russian liberal opposition as it was possible for
a Western journalist to be, earlier in the war he was susceptible to
some of the worst prejudices of the Russian establishment. For
example, in 1915 the professor commented uncritically that 'Jews in
the Polish border areas have been removed from some military
centres where they have given assistance to the enemy', forgetting
the patriotic speeches of Jewish leaders which he had committed to
his diary only months earlier.

Behind this remark lay episodes of mass evictions, shootings and
hangings carried out on the civilian Jewish population by the
Russian military on the orders of the Chief of Staff General N. N.
Yanushkevich. The campaign of mass evacuation at a few hours'
notice, and firing squads for 'spies' and 'enemy agents' after
summary trials, was launched as early as the autumn of 1914, as the
Russian Army began its retreat in Poland, Galicia and the Bukovina.
In terms that foreshadow the later narrative of a much greater
catastrophe, the Russian liberal and Jewish press carried blood-
curdling accounts of sealed rail transports lasting days and of people
dying en route, of towns being entirely cleared of their Jews at
twenty-four hours notice, and those who failed to leave being
handed over to the military authorities for field courts martial.
Leaving behind all their property, which was immediately looted,

and often denied any form of transport, men and women, old and young, and children, including babes-in-arms, were commonly made to trudge eastwards to the next town, which they found closed to them, and were then forced to continue their trek all through the icy winter night. The numbers affected were astronomical: 150,000 and 50,000 from the Lithuanian provinces of Kovno and Grodno, while from Russian Poland the figure was 200,000.

Unaware of the treatment being meted out by the Turks to the Armenian population of Anatolia at this time, and incapable of imagining what would befall them in the 1940s, the Jews in Russia thought the tsarist regime had finally abandoned all restraint and had resolved on a final solution of the 'Jewish Question'. The Duma heard a long account by a peasant deputy, now a soldier, who had witnessed the treatment of the entire Jewish population of the north-western provinces. Altogether, he estimated, half a million people were treated like animals and condemned to suffering. Some governors had seized identity papers and issued passes with time limits stamped in them, prolonging the agony of homelessness and forced wandering. To add further misery, the authorities also took hostages, mostly rabbis and wealthy merchants, whose lives were forfeit in case of treachery by any part of the Jewish population. All these facts and commentaries were assiduously translated and published by Lucien Wolf in his newsletter *Darkest Russia*, as well as by socialist groups and the Yiddish press in London. The Jews in Britain knew about the situation in Russia and were appalled.

As if Wolf's newsletter were not enough, Jewish communities in America – still neutral and still the Mecca for Russian-Jewish refugees, if only they could reach it – were learning at first hand of the plight of their brethren in Russia. The persecution generated a wave of would-be émigrés, not thousands, but certainly hundreds, and the authorities at Archangel, the only European Russian port that remained open throughout the summer months of the war years, reported that their city was overcrowded with refugees seeking passage. As much affected by anti-Semitic hysteria as most other cities in the Russian north-west, Archangel recoiled from the influx of people whose reputation of 'disloyalty' had preceded them, and the local authorities took steps to ensure the Jews did not enter the city proper. Huts were built at a camp at the nearby mainline railhead of Isakagorka where the refugees could await the ships that would take them from the port area of Bakaritsa to America.

In August 1915 Assistant Secretary to the Council of Ministers, A. M. Yakhontov, reported that the Allied governments were expressing disquiet at what was going on. The Russian government had repeatedly tried to curb Yanushkevich's excesses, making it clear to him that domestic and foreign policy considerations needed to be taken into account. But they pleaded in vain. Yakhontov told the ministers that the local mood had assumed an increasingly alarming character:

> The Jews have a grudge against all and sundry, and the local people resent both the uninvited guests, who in any case are branded as traitors and spies, and also the intolerable deterioration in their own living conditions. The Jewish intelligentsia and Russian public opinion, which is at one with them, are indignant to the highest degree; the press, the Duma parties, various organisations, individual prominent representatives of Russian Jewry are demanding ... decisive action to stop this mass persecution ... In Allied countries, and especially in America ... protest meetings are taking place against ethnic persecution ... As a result, we are experiencing increasing difficulty in obtaining funds both on the internal and foreign markets.

Yakhontov pointed out that even inveterate anti-Semites came to members of the government with protests and complaints concerning 'the revolting treatment of Jews at the front'.

The flow of refugees seeking to leave Russia and congregating in the Archangel area while they waited for the thaw and the possibility of a ship, continued until May 1916, when the military commandant of Archangel requested urgent orders from the ministry of the interior prohibiting the further departure of emigrants from Archangel. 'Given their impoverished state, the shipment of those who are already here will be the last.' No figures exist for the total numbers involved, but it was sufficient to prompt the US administration to ask the Russian government to halt the shipments.

Minister of the Interior Shcherbatov warned the government that the 'semi-demented' Yanushkevich was stirring up a pogrom mood among his soldiers who had been egged on by their commander to 'beat the Yids!' The Chief of Staff was following a plan to inflame the army's prejudice against all Jews indiscriminately and to blame them for the setbacks at the front. Shcherbatov stated bluntly: '...Yanushkevich is using the Jews as a scapegoat ...' He urged the government to defuse the mounting tension in the interior and to deflect the criticism of its policies coming both from Russian liberals and Allied governments. The government was divided on the issue and some ministers were swayed by the information that the Germans, allegedly acting in the interests of the German Zionists, had made efforts to recruit the help of Jews in the frontier zones, and were even hoping to instigate an armed uprising against the Russian Army's rear. Weighing up the pros and cons of the situation, the government opted for a compromise: it adopted Shcherbatov's proposal to relax the restrictions on Jewish residence for the duration of the war only, with the proviso that Jews not be permitted to reside in rural communities. In other words, the conditions of Jewish residence inside the Pale were extended to the whole of Russia – a genuine concession. In addition, restraints on entrance to high school and universities were eased, in particular for the children of Jews engaged on war work. The Jews could have been forgiven for thinking that their Russian future might after all become brighter under the tsarist regime.

But, chastened by this experience, the army command, long after the removal of Yanushkevich to a safer command in the Caucasus, turned to policies which, they believed, were less likely to attract outside attention, but which nonetheless would keep up the morale of the troops: again the Jews were targeted as the internal enemy.

Russian military intelligence reported in November 1915 that the job of feeding workers who were digging trenches had been handed over by the army to the *Zemstvo* Union, that is, the voluntary or 'public' body which coordinated the civilian sector's contribution to the war effort; and it had further been noted that in some canteens the staff was made up entirely of Jews. It was felt wrong to have such people in these places, first because 'they could steal the plans for the trenches' and, second, because they could easily agitate the trench workers who were dissatisfied with the government; and finally these wretches had been fed so badly that some of them had come down with infectious diseases. Then, to cope with the local shortage of sugar for the troops, quartermasters were instructed to buy sweets of equivalent sugar-content from Christian firms only, 'as the confectionary made by Jewish manufacturers may be harmful'.

The accusations became ever more strident. At the beginning of

December 1915 the intelligence service reported that the *Zemstvo* Union was employing Jews who were either evading military service or trying to penetrate the ranks of the army where they would conduct 'party agitation'. The new Chief of Staff General Mikhail Alekseyev ordered that if sapper teams supplied by the Union could not be made up without Jews, then the army must do without them altogether. In January 1916 the Police Department informed all governors and chief administrators that intelligence reports showed that the Jews were engaged in redoubled revolutionary activity among the troops and in large industrial enterprises, and were inciting strikes by artificially inflating the price of essential goods and causing the disappearance of small currency.

An upsurge in factory unrest in early 1916, which, if it was at all organised, was organised by the few Russian Social Democrats still at large in the capital, was blamed on Jewish revolutionaries by an intelligence service that knew what its political masters wished to hear. It reported that the Germans were 'well aware that the mood of the Russian people had not been adversely affected either by the army's failures or by revolutionary agitation', and so now the revolutionaries, 'together with their Jewish inspirers and pro-German sympathisers', were out to provoke general discontent, an anti-war protest movement by means of hunger and a steep rise in the cost of essential goods. Bloody-minded tradesmen were allegedly hiding goods, slowing down deliveries, holding up the loading of food at railway stations. By hoarding small currency the Jews were trying to undermine the people's confidence in Russian paper money, causing them to withdraw their savings and to hoard metal money. (The fact that paper money was fast losing its value under rampant inflation was ignored.) Jewish efforts to abolish the Pale, it was claimed, were aimed at spreading their criminal and seditious activities into Russia proper, where they would create the sort of disorder from which only the Jews themselves could profit.

In February 1916 Lieutenant General Evgeny Miller, acting commander of 5th Army in the Baltic provinces, forbade the use of Jewish soldiers in signals units altogether, whether as telegraphists or telephonists or checkers, but especially not as clerks. This order was to be carried out within seven days by unit commanders who were charged, on pain of court-martial, with informing HQ that it had been done. The head of the Minsk gendarmes reported in March that Russian and Polish engineers employed by the Union of Towns and *Zemstvos* were becoming restive and were showing hostility towards Jews, 'who everywhere occupy the cushiest jobs, worm their way in as assistants to the directors and carry on intrigues, are obviously hostile to the war and the strengthening of the rear, saying that all our efforts will come to nothing and often hint at the ineffectiveness of the High Command. Only the *Zemstvo* staff support the Jews, while the engineers and the other specialists are against them ... they say the Jews are harmful and dangerous to the Russian people'.

In August, the commander of the 175th Reserve Regiment ordered that Jewish troops of the lower ranks who had passed through basic training should be sent to front-line units as soon as possible, and that the first contingents should consist entirely of Jews on the basis of seniority – that is, the most experienced should go first.

The campaign of anti-Jewish slander, in implicating the voluntary organisations, sought to achieve several goals at once: to stifle criticism of the regime for the breakdown of the domestic economy and the inflation that had decimated the value of the rouble; to discredit the voluntary organisations which were perceived, with some justice, to be laying the foundations for their own political future through patriotic good works and at the cost of the reputation of the military; to nip in the bud Jewish ambitions for the full equality they anticipated as their reward, whether from the tsarist regime or its successor.

The army command seems to have been carrying on the war on three fronts, one against the Central Powers, another against the voluntary bodies and a third against the Jews. It was of course of great convenience to a losing leadership – especially one steeped in the defensive mentality that dominated it after the 1905 Revolution – that all three enemies could be linked by the common purpose of bringing down the tsarist regime. And in a sense there was indeed such a 'conspiracy' to topple the Romanov dynasty: the Russian revolutionary movement was well populated with Jews, the liberals in the Duma and the *zemstvos* were the Jews' allies in their struggle for civil equality, while in the army the Jewish troops – about 600,000 of them in the course of the war, some 200,000 in mid-1917 – were just as susceptible as the rest of the army to the war fatigue that in the summer of 1917 would provide the soil for Lenin's defeatist propaganda.

As civilians became more involved in voluntary work at the front, so the government's handling of the war came under closer scrutiny, and both the authorities and the voluntary bodies alike felt that the war itself had provided a new arena of political struggle. It was axiomatic among all sections of society that the interests of the Russian Jews and those of the progressive reformers coincided: Jewish civil rights would only be achieved through participation in the liberal constitutionalist movement. Hence, even after General Yanushkevich's departure, the Jews continued to serve as a stalking-horse for the military in their troubled relationship with the voluntary bodies.

Since the autumn of 1915 the military had been badgering the Chief Committee of Russian Town Unions to dismiss all its Jewish workers from all front activities, with the exception of doctors. The Committee rebuffed this assault on its principles, as well as its efficiency, and in March 1916 organised a protest directly to the Tsar and the Duma. The Jewish members of the organisations saw the new regulations as a device to sow dissension in the public bodies, and, more importantly from the Jewish point of view, to turn the Jews into a wedge dividing government and society. Until the new orders were withdrawn, the Jewish voluntary workers found it morally impossible to work on any part of the front where there were restrictions on Jews. The suspicion of provocation was well-founded. A report from the commander of the Sanitary Division to 10th Army in East Prussia prompted its HQ to order the *Zemstvo* Union to dismiss all Jews from their service: 'If the administration of the Union does not comply with this proposal', the sanitary commander was told, 'you must not accept the services of the Union, as the utility of the Union's work does not exceed the harm caused by the admission of spying Jews to the service of the Union.'

Spying was not the only offence the Jews were accused of in the front-line zone. The authorities on the South-Western Front learnt that the number of soldiers ill with venereal diseases, especially syphilis, had greatly increased, and they alleged that a German-Jewish organisation was spending large sums of money on prostitutes whose task it was to infect Russian officers. A watch on all hotels, furnished rooms and 'suspicious private houses' was ordered, and any women found to be infected were to be 'mercilessly punished by administrative means', forcibly placed in hospital and deported to remote regions of the empire. If they were found to belong to any suspect organisation, they were to be subjected to corporal punishment and then deported.

While Russian officers were allegedly victims of sexual subversion, the number of Russian troops reporting with self-inflicted injuries was growing. Military intelligence also reported the apparent existence of a criminal organisation whose agents, 'chiefly Jews', were trying to impose on the Poles the idea that Poles need no longer serve in the Russian Army on the grounds that the Germans had restored all the damage they had caused in Poland, that Kaiser Wilhelm's brother was to become King of Poland, and that therefore Polish soldiers returning home wearing Russian uniform would be unwelcome. They would be well advised, in other words, to join the growing numbers of those who were deserting the Russian Army.

The mass evacuations from the front-line zones, the daily spectacle of hangings and executions by firing squad, and the torrent of allegations and accusations had two objectives. The first aim was to repeat the successful policy that had bolstered Russian national unity after the assassination of Alexander II in 1881, and again after the calamity of 1905, by deflecting mass discontent onto 'the enemy within'. After 1905 the target had been the revolutionaries and the Jews. In 1915–16 the most prominent and active revolutionaries were either abroad or in Siberian exile and could no longer serve as a target. The ethnically un-Russian area of the Polish and Galician frontiers more readily swallowed the allegation that Russia was being stabbed in the back by those who allegedly hated everything Russian, namely the Jews.

The second aim of the campaign was to subvert the unity and success of the voluntary organisations which had been established to aid the war effort, only after great personal pressure had been exerted on Nicholas II. The transfer of Yanushkevich to the Caucasus in August 1915 was prompted by the foreign press campaign against the barbarities of the Russian Army in defeat, and it took place at a time by which the vaunted national unity of August 1914 had all but evaporated. Opposition politicians were loudly calling on the government to shed its distrust of society and to allow politicians and industrialists and the *zemstvos* to shoulder a share of the burden. The government's competence and the role of the Tsar were now coming under open attack. It was precisely at this moment, the summer of 1915, that in a fit of misjudged zeal the Tsar assumed the position of Supreme Commander. Leaving the domestic running of the country and control of the ministers in the hands of his wife, he took up his position at General Headquarters. This mindless decision gave his political enemies much of the ammunition they would use to bring about his downfall.

By 1915 the unhealed wounds of 1905 had reopened, with the difference now that the war was not a distant event in the Far East, the enemy was more formidable, Russia now had allies who were making demands that stretched her capacities, greater strains were placed on her economy, and the regime finally had to resign itself to coming to some sort of working arrangement with the vocal forces of opposition and reform.

Well before 1914 the educated classes had lost whatever illusions they may have retained that Nicholas II was the man to save Russia from drifting into a political backwater. A catalogue of failure – the 1905 Revolution, defeat by Japan, the half-hearted concession of a pseudo-parliament, which the government repeatedly and cynically manipulated, scandals at court and the royal family's degradation at the hands of their 'friend' Rasputin – all this had reduced the image of Nicholas II from that of an elevated autocrat to an all-too-human being, widely rumoured to be attached to the vodka bottle – anything but a divinely appointed sovereign. Leaving aside the transient display of devotion shown to the Tsar by all classes at his public appearances – most graphically by front-line troops piously on their knees before him – the public mood was increasingly republican. This was clearly demonstrated after his abdication in February/March 1917: with the monarchists lying low in justified fear of the anarchy on the streets, the crucial question of whether to continue fighting or leave the war was not discussed in terms of whether or not the monarchy should be reinstated. It was over the Russian *republic* that the contending parties fought in the months leading up to the Bolshevik seizure of power in October/November and would continue to fight in the civil war that followed.

The disaffection of the educated classes was matched among the lower classes by the sullen mood that descended once again on the troops after the defeats of 1914 and 1915. Ill-equipped and, as they came to see it, ill-led, Russian soldiers were driven into battle purely by military discipline. They had enthusiasm neither for the war nor for the regime that ordered them to defend it.

The Jews, meanwhile, were being advertised as shirkers from military service, as instigators of food shortages and inflation, makers of industrial strife, agents of dissension and disaffection in the ranks, purveyors of trench plans and telephone messages to the enemy, poisoners of the food, carriers of venereal diseases in the brothels used by Russian officers. In this catalogue of indictment, which accentuated their identity as utterly alien, the Jews of Russia were excluded from Russia's national interest. The horror stories published by Lucien Wolf in *Darkest Russia* made all this plain. The underlying message for the Russian Jews of Britain was that joining the British Army was the right thing to do.

Privately the British government knew that Russia did not want its Jews back, for military or any other purposes. This was a fact that could not be made public. Instead, the game was played of seeking a solution that would satisfy British public opinion and save the face of Anglo-Jewry. Although the government could not say so openly, it had implicitly accepted that the Russian Jews ought not to be sent back to Tsarist Russia. If the French, Belgian and Italian immigrants had been returned to their native lands, it was partly because those countries had wanted them back, but also because none of them could claim to have been hounded out of their homelands by their own government, and because they themselves wished it. The British government had a clear understanding of this.*

The point was sharpened when the issue of reciprocity was raised. If Russians were to be sent back into the Russian Army, the 500 British men of military age resident in Russia would be expected to serve in the Russian Army or face deportation. At once the absurdity of the comparison became obvious: the threat of deportation for Russian Jews was to be matched by the privilege of repatriation for British subjects! The best answer Herbert Samuel could give to the question of whether it was legitimate to enlist aliens was that he knew the Russian government had not objected to the idea of their subjects joining Allied armies, and that this was the guiding principle of British policy.

This question had really only arisen in France, since only there were there comparable numbers of Russians, again mostly Jews. But what the Home Secretary did not tell the House – he may not even have known it – was that the exiled Russian revolutionaries in Paris had greeted the outbreak of the war with an outburst of enthusiasm.

---

* E.g. Italians in Canada organised their own return, without prompting from any government.

The history of Bolshevism itself is embarrassed by this show of zeal for the war by the most internationalist of communities, although it was not only Bolsheviks who were aroused to defend freedom and democracy. No figures of party affiliation are known, except that the recruiting secretary, the recruiting halls and the recruitment manifesto were all provided by the Bolsheviks. Singing revolutionary songs, more than 9,000 Russians – revolutionaries and non-political émigrés – passed through the Paris recruitment office on 21 August 1914, and next day nearly 4,000 men who had been found fit for action were sent off to camp and the front.

This glorious moment faded when the volunteers discovered that aliens who wished to fight for the Allied cause were not to be sent to the French Army, whose motto was 'Honour and Fatherland', but to the French Foreign Legion, whose motto was 'Honour and Discipline'. The Foreign Legion, especially in wartime, regarded itself as beyond the norms of ordinary military conduct, and life there has been compared unfavourably with that of a penitentiary. 'Any man who comes to the Legion should know that he comes to die, or at least that there is small hope of escape', the Legion's recruiting sergeants promised. Reflecting the secular character of French state institutions in general, and affording Jewish legionnaires a degree of reassurance, the Legion's discharge book, unlike its Russian equivalent, contained no mention of a man's religion or national origin.

While concealing the fact that Russian exiles and émigrés were being pursued by the authorities to serve the Allied cause, on 11 July 1916 Lord Cecil of the Foreign Office told Joseph King that the Russian government had *not* asked for eligible Russians to be sent back, repeating this on 18 December, but confirming that discussions were continuing. On 13 February 1917, the Foreign Office reported that the Russian government was now ready to sign an agreement. The process was interrupted by the abdication of Nicholas II a month later and the demise of the old regime.

4 Revolutionaries Abroad

With the growth of the Russian-Jewish immigrant population in Western Europe and the United States came increasing awareness of the condition of Jews in the Russian Empire. Protest and defence organisations were set up to lobby governments and to inform public opinion. In London, for example, the Conjoint Foreign Committee and its moving spirit, Lucien Wolf, kept up pressure on the Foreign Office not to ignore the deteriorating position of the Jews in Russia. For Western Jews the difficulty was to draw a distinction between demonstrating their complete identification with the country of their citizenship and their claim to speak with moral authority on behalf of their brethren in 'Darkest Russia'. For Western governments, the difficulty was where to draw the line between remaining friendly with another power and interfering in its domestic policies in order to satisfy the demands of a particular group.

During wartime, it was reasonable to expect that Russia would be sensitive to public opinion in Allied countries and would respond by repudiating and suppressing the accusations of treachery as depicted in *Darkest Russia*. But from the Allies' point of view, the Jewish question was bound to be seen as secondary to the need to bolster Russia's morale and her war effort. It was unrealistic of Jewish activists in the West to expect their governments to do otherwise. In January 1917, the Foreign Office told Jewish leaders that nothing could be done to extend to the Russian Jews 'the liberty and justice' for which the Allies were fighting. The British Foreign Secretary, Arthur Balfour, shared the general view that the Jewish question, like all other questions of liberty and justice, would be settled in Russia by the abolition of the old order as a result of an Allied victory.

The Anglo-Jewish position was in danger of being compromised. Years of hostility towards Russia over the Jewish question made it seem that Anglo-Jewish establishment figures, many of them bearing German names, might adopt a pro-German or at least a neutral position. Their refusal to join in the clamour of anti-German sentiment and their inclination to urge the movement for peace did little to strengthen the Jewish leadership's hand with the British government. The *Jewish Chronicle* protested on the eve of the war against the squandering of British resources and the spilling of British blood 'in order that the Slavs may maintain their position against the Teutons and an effete and barbarous autocracy be sustained on a tottering throne. We have no interest in the upholding of Russia and far less the debasing of Germany' with whom Britain had no quarrel whatsoever. Given this attitude, it is remarkable that the Jewish leadership ever managed to get back into the corridors of Whitehall, let alone the confidence of the government.

Defeatism was not a sentiment to be heard in Britain at war. The importance of the British Empire as a world power, and its vast scale which had been impressed on every child at school, rendered defeatism an untenable political position. Conscientious objection, pacifism and anti-war sentiment were, however, well-developed movements among intellectuals and left-wing trade unionists.

According to reports given to the tsarist secret police by its agents 'Amerikanets' and 'Weber', who were watching the activities of the Russian revolutionaries in London, propaganda in favour of a Russian defeat was being spread among English workers, especially in the munitions factories of Woolwich Arsenal and Vickers. 'Amerikanets' informed the Paris headquarters of the Russian secret police (*Okhrana*) in August 1916 that the Russian revolutionaries – using a Committee for Russian Prisoners' Relief as a front – conducted propaganda in English society and among the organised proletariat against the alliance of 'free England and tsarist Russia', and at the same time carried on 'internationalist' agitation inside workers' organisations. With access to certain newspapers, especially the *Cotton Factory Times* and *The Call*, which openly advertised itself as 'an organ of International Socialism', the revolutionary agitators were even using primitive – and inaccurate – etymology to convince English workers of the danger of an alliance with the Russians: 'A nation of slaves, slavery is in the very soul of every Russian, and even the name, Slav, comes from the Assyrian meaning "slave", and such people wish to be ruled by a stronger force. A German victory can only improve and delight the condition of the British people.'*

---

* 'Slav' in fact derives from the Greek word *Sklavos*, and denotes a language group.

'Amerikanets' went on to say that the workers at Woolwich and Vickers had become more involved in the work of the committee – 'a purely Jewish group' – which sought to exploit this interest. One of the group, a Socialist Revolutionary called Makushin, reported that he had had to listen to such unlikely tales about Russia, told to the workers by 'the Jew Chicherin', that he could only throw up his hands in the end and leave that 'Jewish company'. The report concluded, 'Makushin, who was incidentally the only real Russian on the Committee, once protested and was immediately attacked by the majority for displaying patriotism'.

The designation of Georgy Chicherin as a Jew reflects several aspects of the atmosphere of the time: it simplified the political profile of the anti-war group in the agent's report, as underlined by the only 'real' Russian's disgust; it confirmed the widely held belief that the Russian Jews were pursuing a policy of their own; it detached the Jews from any clear interest of state and reinforced their image as cosmopolitans who would exploit any situation to their own advantage, hence Makushin's response as a *Russian* revolutionary, that is, one with a *national* revolutionary interest; and finally it confirmed that the anti-war position was really an anti-Russian position and that those who adopted it were working for the Germans.

The image of the Russian Jews as detached and anti-Russian at the same time is graphically illustrated in the memoirs of Alexander Shlyapnikov. He was an engineering worker, not a Jew but a Russian Bolshevik of great value to Lenin and the Bolshevik cause during the war, an intrepid wartime traveller in and out of Petrograd, via England and Scandinavia. He relates in his memoirs that when Nikolai Bukharin, another 'real Russian' Bolshevik, and his wife came from Switzerland to London in 1915, he travelled on the passport of a Jew in order to present a 'non-national' image. And as he had attracted the hostile attention of French and English anti-Semites the ploy evidently worked. But when Shlyapnikov applied to the Russian Consulate in London during the same summer for a visa to travel to Russia, he remarks that his '"genuine" Russian physiognomy provoked no suspicions, and a stamp was placed in my passport for the exit'. So, travelling around Western Europe during the war was easier for the Russian Bukharin if he posed as a cosmopolitan Jew, but getting into Russia with anything but a plainly Russian face would raise doubts about one's purpose.

The police spy was not so far off the mark about the ethnic composition of the London group, as almost everyone in it was indeed a Russian Jew. And the Bolsheviks, who were the explicitly defeatist wing of the international socialist movement, had recognised the revolutionary potential in the Russian-Jewish question. During his stay in Russia from the summer of 1915 to June 1916, Shlyapnikov gathered a rich collection of materials on the position of the Russian Jews in war conditions, with the aim of printing a pamphlet on the subject for Western Jewish consumption. Shlyapnikov recalled that Jews in Stockholm expressed an interest in his material when he showed it to them on his way to the United States, but he decided not to sell it to them, fearing it might fall into the hands of the German General Staff who could use it for their own ends. Instead he took it with him to New York, where 'the Russian colony was enormous, two daily papers were published, (including a social democratic one in Russian) and several other papers in Yiddish and other languages'.

Under-funded bodies were not Shlyapnikov's target of choice: 'With regard to my own business, I learnt that I had not chosen altogether the most propitious time to arrive. All the rich Jewish community had gone off for the summer ...' As in Stockholm, he resisted selling his wares to blatantly pro-German parties, and sought instead a clearly anti-Russian lobby, although he states that the only condition he imposed on a prospective purchaser was that the material should be passed on to any Jewish organisation that would publish it in English and other languages. After a couple of months, and in the absence of any rich Jews, Shlyapnikov still managed to settle for the then considerable sum of $500 from some 'Jewish scholars', half of which he would need to get himself back to Russia, the other half he would use for revolutionary work once he got there. Shlyapnikov's whole operation had been conceived with the approval of Lenin, whose only concern had been whether money for the trip could be found: it was taken for granted that getting material on the situation in Russia into the right hands, for an anti-Russian campaign in the American press, was a good thing to do. The path to the Revolution was, however, paved with good intentions, and in the end Shlyapnikov's material never saw the light of day.

American attitudes to the war were very different from British attitudes. Neutral until April 1917, when the US entered the war on the side of the Allies the American population included sizeable minorities from all sides of the conflict, each of them with their own perspective on the war, neutralism being the only common denominator. Among Jewish radicals in New York the shared currency was the hope for a Russian defeat, though not a German victory. Whether or not consciously echoing Lenin's thesis, that the defeat of Russia would be a 'lesser evil' than a German victory, the Yiddish-language Anarchist New York paper *Freier Arbeiter Shtimme* (Free Workers' Voice) asserted in late 1914: 'No matter how terrible German imperialism may be, the Jews of Russia would profit politically, economically, and above all spiritually from a Russian defeat.' Such expressions of defeatism continued unabated in the USA as long as the country remained outside the war.

Jewish radical opinion in America was in fact predominantly defeatist, as far as Russia was concerned. As many as 75 per cent of the Jewish intellectual leaders in New York had been active in the Russian revolutionary movement before they emigrated, and they knew that political progress, such as it was, had been made after 1905 because of Russia's defeat at the hands of the Japanese. The same would be true of this war, they were convinced. A Russian victory, on the other hand, would only secure the continuation of the Romanov autocracy. It was a view also held by Russian liberals, not that they wished or worked for a Russian defeat, rather that they feared for democracy's future in the event of a Russian victory with Nicholas II still at the head of the armed forces and his position strengthened.

Jewish radicals in America viewed England (synonymous with Britain) and France sympathetically – France as the cradle of liberty and England as a model of the civil society. There was considerable pro-German feeling among certain American Jewish circles, notably the most prosperous of German origin, but again they were chiefly moved by deep hostility to the anti-Semitic government of Russia. Virtually all of American-Jewish opinion before the spring of 1917, whether pro-German or pro-Allied, was anti-Russian.

* * *

The terms 'Russian Jews' and 'immigrant community' conceal one of the most extraordinary features of the Russian Jews in Britain – their occupational profile. Apart from the (non-Jewish) Lithuanian coal-miners of Lanarkshire in Scotland, no other group of immigrants or refugees was as concentrated in a single industry as the Russian Jews. Certainly there were cabinet-makers and shoemakers in large numbers, powder-puff makers and watchmakers aplenty, but it was above all in the clothing industry, and in particular tailoring, that Russian Jews were employed in large numbers. The world they had left behind was that of the small workshop, and in London and Leeds they now inhabited a working world that was strikingly similar.

At a time when 'bespoke tailoring' for men and women was coming onto the market at relatively affordable prices, the demand for tailors was insatiable. In the London of 1915 alone, out of 65,000 tailors, male and female, about 20,000 were Jews, of whom a majority were Russian aliens. Leeds, dubbed 'the London of the North', had proportionally comparable numbers. Of London's total tailoring workforce, only about 8,000 were unionised, and of these nearly 6,000 were Jews. Small workshops, in England as in Russia, made it difficult to unionise. Often the master tailor's wife and children worked for him, and he himself might easily become someone else's hired workman in a poor season. Union membership therefore prevailed in the bigger workshops. In addition, the statistics include many men and women who were transient, stopping over and working in London only until they were able to move on to the United States. Between 1881 and 1911, about 200,000 Russian Jews arrived in London, but only 105,000 to 120,000 settled permanently. Transient workers were least likely to join a union, if only because union membership, as they knew it, might attract police attention and complicate the task of preparing for the onward trek.

Although union membership was not a prerequisite of political agitation, among the Conventionists who went back in the summer of 1917 were the politically committed, and a side effect of their departure was the decimation of political parties in London, such as the Bund. The working men who thronged meetings and clubs were not all union members: union membership presupposed concern with economic grievances; political agitation, particularly against the war, was the concern of everyone, especially men of military age. And it was in such surroundings, more than in the hectic rush of the workplace, that Russian-Jewish workers came under the influence of articulate radicals and Russian revolutionaries.

The war had a devastating effect on the Russian revolutionary community abroad. It split the movement into those who supported Russia's defence and those who did not. For the 'defensists', the war was a contest between the Western democracies and German militarism, and for them a German victory meant an inevitable setback for progress to socialism. The fact that the democracies were allied with reactionary tsarist Russia had to be swallowed, and anyway the war – it was hoped – would so weaken Russia that tsarism would be no match for the forces of progress. Opponents of the war were further divided into 'internationalists' who advocated every means to achieve a peace 'without indemnities or annexations' – a so-called 'non-imperialist' peace – and a small minority who actively worked for a tsarist defeat as the prelude to socialist revolution in Russia first, and then all of Europe (and the world) thereafter. The defeatists' chief spokesman was Lenin.

A further effect was brought about by the geography of the war. Paris had traditionally been the chief continental centre of the Russian revolutionary movement abroad, a fact recognised by the tsarist secret police, who as early as 1887 had set up a large establishment there to keep the Russian communities under surveillance and to intercept foreign mail on its way to Russia. Although Paris remained important as an émigré centre, during the war only neutral Switzerland and Scandinavia were safe havens for revolutionaries who preached defeatism. From Switzerland, surrounded as it was by belligerents, it was virtually impossible to make illegal journeys to Russia, or elsewhere, whereas Scandinavia, with its long coastline, numerous shipping outlets and countless archipelagos, provided an excellent substitute, and a certain amount of traffic managed to get into Russia via that northern route. Britain, therefore, with its sea links to Scandinavia, became relatively more important.

London had always presented Russian exiles with a more provincial perspective than Paris or Zurich. Ivan Maisky, who spent many years in London before and during the war, and who was to return in 1932 as Soviet ambassador, notes in his memoirs that Russian exiles found it much easier to lie low among London's vast population, and that their only difficulty in maintaining regular contact with each other arose from the greater distances they had to travel across the capital. The availability of work, especially for the workers among the exiles, and the more relaxed attitude of the English towards politics generally, made for a less stressful, if less exciting life than in Paris.

Lenin's man in London, and Stalin's future foreign commissar, was Maxim Litvinov. Born in Belostok in 1876 to a minor Jewish merchant family called Vallakh, Litvinov became a Marxist revolutionary in 1898 during his military service in the Russian Army. Soon after discharge, he became an illegal activist in the Bolshevik 'underground', smuggling literature and people into Russia. During the 1905 Revolution he ran a shipment of what turned out to be rusty and useless guns for an armed uprising which was staged and savagely crushed in Moscow. In 1908 he was arrested in Paris, not for the first time, while attempting to exchange roubles stolen in a bank robbery in Tiflis, Georgia, which Stalin had masterminded on Lenin's orders. Litvinov then moved to London where he worked as a clerk for a publisher. He acquired not only excellent idiomatic English but also an English wife, Ivy Lowe, the daughter of a Hungarian-Jewish journalist who had changed the family name from Loewe upon arrival in England as a political refugee, converted to Anglicanism and become a successful small businessman.

Settled into family and working life in London, Litvinov's job as Lenin's agent was to establish links in the British labour movement and among factory workers, and to try to promote the defeatist cause. Given the prevailing attitudes of the English, this was a hopeless task, but as both Special Branch and Russian secret police files show, Litvinov was adept at infiltrating the workshops of munitions plants, even if he failed to dent the defensive mentality of most of his would-be converts. Litvinov went back to Russia as a political émigré in the summer before the October Revolution, returning to Britain in January 1918 as the new Soviet government's first envoy.

A more important role in anti-conscription agitation was played by Georgy Chicherin, mistakenly identified in the 'Amerikanets' report as a Jew. Descended from an Italian courtier in fifteenth-century Muscovy named Cicerini, Chicherin was socially several cuts above the average Russian revolutionary, even those of gentry origin, like Lenin, to say nothing of such sons of simple Jewish folk as Litvinov and most if not all of the rest. His Russian ancestors included statesmen, generals and most notably his Uncle Boris, a great legal philosopher and inspirer of the nineteenth-century liberal constitutionalist movement, and on whose estate Georgy was born in 1872. His mother's family were the Meyendorffs and Shtakelbergs, the crème de la crème of the elite Baltic German families which provided so many of Russia's diplomats. Fittingly, in 1897 Georgy followed his father into the foreign ministry – the most aristocratic of the services – where he worked in the tranquil confines of the archives. Seven years later, as student riots, peasant outbreaks, workers' demonstrations and the effects of the Russo-Japanese War were raising the political pressure to storm force, Chicherin suddenly experienced a deep emotional crisis, though its cause or causes have not been discovered or disclosed. In Bolshevik literature he is commonly described as being 'extremely refined' and of a 'sickly disposition', a view which may reflect the prevailing prejudice against homosexuals of the period. But though in the foreign ministry he remained 'in the closet', in St Petersburg's artistic and theatrical circles he was relaxed and open about his sexual preference.

It was common practice at that time for homosexuals to seek medical help, and Chicherin duly attended Dr Lehr's nerve clinic in Berlin. There, according to the authorised version, he was attracted by the Bolsheviks, their militancy, their openness about the need to try to seize power should the opportunity arise, and he joined them. In the period following the collapse of the 1905 Revolution, Lenin's rivals, the Mensheviks, followed a more conciliatory path. They dealt openly with organised labour and, after a brief lapse, made the most of the political concessions that had been wrested from the tsarist regime in the 1905 Revolution, and helped the working class to achieve 'political consciousness' and enter the political arena. In stark contrast, Lenin's Bolsheviks engaged in bank robberies and gun-running in collaboration with the Socialist Revolutionaries, who were in effect the terrorist branch of the Russian revolutionary movement.

The split of the Russian Social Democratic Party into Bolsheviks and Mensheviks in 1903 had not been well received by the party rank and file, who on the whole viewed it as the self-indulgent hair-splitting of intellectuals, and it had given rise to a strong sentiment for party unity that was reinforced by the defeat of the 1905 Revolution. The Bolsheviks and Mensheviks in exile in Berlin managed to unite, and by 1907 Chicherin had become a Menshevik.

When the war broke out, Chicherin was in Belgium, organising protests against voluntary enlistment by Russian émigrés. Confusingly, he wrote in a letter of December 1914 that he regarded the anti-recruitment movement as 'disarming the democracy in the face of advancing despotism, and all those who aid the destruction of the Western democracies are *de facto* enemies

of socialism'. In another letter to a fellow Menshevik, he ridiculed
Lenin's view that the bourgeois system was in its death throes. As
for Lenin's call to the proletariat to revolt, he thought this was
living in a 'confusion of dream and reality' which rested on 'airy
foundations'.* By July 1916 this man of vacillating views and little
certainty was the driving force in the anti-conscription movement in
London, heading a committee which included men and women
regardless of party affiliation.

Chicherin's transition back from Menshevik to Bolshevik is not
clear to see. He himself wrote that the war played havoc with the
factional loyalties of revolutionaries, himself included, and there are
many instances where party divisions were ignored. The issue of
party loyalty did not become critical until the middle of 1917. In any
event, Maisky remarks that in 1916 Chicherin was not yet a
Bolshevik, nor had he formally broken with the Mensheviks. And
Chicherin himself was suitably vague. It is perhaps enough to say
that he followed an internationalist line and that after his forcibly
delayed return to Russia in January 1918, he would succeed Trotsky
in March 1918 as Soviet Commissar for Foreign Affairs.

In London Chicherin soon became involved in fund-raising for
political prisoners in Russia, finding allies in the British Socialist
Party and the anti-war Left of the British labour movement. He
was at once spotted by the authorities as an undesirable alien.
Special Branch suspected that, as treasurer of the Russian
Prisoners Relief Committee, he was using the funds to foment
strikes in Britain, although they lacked evidence. Maisky
indirectly confirms their suspicions when he writes that, under
Chicherin the committee became a political organisation engaging
in agitation against tsarism: it was a short step from socialist
agitation against tsarism during the war to persuading British
workers that their support of the war only strengthened the forces
of anti-labour reaction.**

In September 1916, a Russian agent reported a meeting at the
Communist Club attended by 40 émigré men, mainly of military age.

---

*   Chicherin's faith in the survival of English capitalism, at least in June 1915,
     encouraged him to take out 'Zeppelin and Accident Insurance' in exchange for
     a daily subscription to *The Daily News*.
**   HO144/2158/322428, 21 October 1916. All references to this file on Chicherin
     carry the same classification and are identified by date only. The file is closed until
     2019 and I was allowed to consult it by kind permission of the Home Office.

The purpose of the meeting was to form an anti-conscription league which would promote a peaceful campaign against compulsory military service for émigrés. They would engage in public meetings and spread the word. American socialist groups in contact with the London socialists were, according to this agent, already 'creating a fuss against the attempt being made on the Jews and émigrés' by the government. Informers had reported that anarchists were even considering armed revenge attacks on English leaders. The émigrés were said to be seriously alarmed at the prospect of conscription and some of them, notably Bolsheviks and anarchists – though not as a group – were determined to resist all the way, including court martial. The strongest protests, understandably, came from those who were wanted for trial back in Russia, among them, despite his influential connections, Chicherin.

Scotland Yard reported to the Home Office that, having at one time been suspected of being in touch with German 'influences', Chicherin was now devoting himself to preventing Jews from enlisting in the army, and on these grounds 'the State Secretary may care to consider deportation'. The Home Office thought that Chicherin's activities among the Russian Jews were no worse than those being pursued by his English friends, Labour people and left-wing MPs, and it was hoped other grounds would be found to get rid of him. In July 1917, at the time the Russian embassy was in contact with the Foreign Office over the repatriation of political exiles, Chicherin wrote an article for Lenin's *Pravda* newspaper, which had resumed publication in Petrograd after the collapse of tsarism in March, in which he claimed the British government was *preventing* Russian political émigrés from going home. The article was translated by MI5 and sent to the Home Office with the comment: 'This strengthens the case for Chicherin's internment. Nearly all the statements in it are untrue.'

The charges on which he was finally arrested in mid-August were for alleged association with Germans and pro-Germans at the Communist Club in Charlotte Street – a favourite haunt of the Russian secret police – and that his anti-Allied and pro-German activities represented a danger to the public safety and the defence of the realm. British security, in short, regarded Chicherin as a Bolshevik in all but name. In the years up to his arrest, Chicherin established an elaborate network of contacts in Britain, including peers and MPs, Labour and trade union leaders, and newspaper editors. Judging by his address book, which is to be found among the Bridges Adams Papers at Columbia University, the majority of his contacts seem to have been Russian Jews and Mensheviks, with a generous sprinkling of British left-wing politicians, such as Ramsay Macdonald and Philip Snowden, members of the Duma, Russian and English journalists and the occasional Russian aristocrat. The absence of Lenin and his wife, Nadezhda Krupskaya – she conducted most of Lenin's correspondence with party organisers and activists – and of any other significant Bolshevik, confirms that Chicherin had no formal organisational link with the Bolsheviks. But he did work closely with Litvinov and he was in touch with non-factional activists in Scandinavia who in 1917 emerged as Bolsheviks.

In all his undertakings Chicherin was assisted by a remarkable Englishwoman called Mrs Mary Bridges Adams,* formerly active on the London Board of Education and now working to protect the right of asylum for refugees. She was uncharitably depicted by Maisky as 'one of those English people who fail somehow to come to terms with life and so devote all their passion and determination to some "cause" which fires their imagination or touches their heart'. When she met Chicherin it was the Russian revolutionary movement that gave her a new cause and she became the moving spirit of the émigré committee. In the eyes of Special Branch, she was just a 'noted peace crank'.

Similar contrasts illustrate the gap in perception that separated those on opposite sides of the political divide. To Maisky, for example, Chicherin was a striking and original personality, innately fastidious, with quick, nervous and unexpected movements which made one think: 'What an interesting man! There is something individual and unusual about him.' Chicherin's relatives in Russia regarded him as completely mad. The newly appointed Russian Consul-General, Onou, whom Chicherin regarded as a potentially useful friend, told Special Branch that Chicherin was 'quite mad and in the hands of Jews and German spies', and that he was a very dangerous man. Onou also divulged that Chicherin had spent some years in the famous Dr Lehr's nerve clinic in Berlin for a serious mental illness – the cause in fact of his failure to join the 1905 Revolution. 'Onou thinks the Russian authorities don't want him back as there were already enough dangerous madmen in Russia.'

---

* The family name was hyphenated by later generations.

Chicherin would die in 1936, not at Stalin's murderous hand, but in a state described as 'clinical madness'.

Languishing in Brixton Prison, south London, Chicherin was refused visits by Joseph King who, although an MP, had been found guilty in October 1916 of communicating secret information (what and to whom was not divulged) and fined £100, or by Mrs Bridges Adams, presumably on grounds of 'undesirability'. He complained that his health was suffering because he had no money to supplement the poor prison diet. Knowing that his family in Russia could not help, he appealed to the Mensheviks to repay money he had lent them in 1907 and again in 1912. And he wrote to Mrs Bridges Adams complaining about 'the lack of marmalade, fruit and golden syrup and other necessities'.

In 1921, when Chicherin was Soviet Foreign Commissar, he received a letter from Mary Bridges Adams in which she complained of being neglected by her now powerful old friends. Alexandra Kollontai had been in London as an emissary of Lenin's and had not even contacted her. She claimed to have financial needs that she had hoped would be met by the Soviet government, no doubt out of their gratitude for services rendered to Chicherin, rather than as payment for current activities. Kollontai wrote to her in the most endearingly regretful terms, pleading lack of time and urgent state business, while Chicherin replied that he had far fewer resources at his disposal than she imagined. Nor, he warned her, should she believe allegations in the English press that Soviet Russia was financing sympathisers of various kinds in the West – allegations which would in fact be vindicated when the Communist Party archives were opened at the end of the 1980s. Nevertheless, he undertook to transmit help of some sort via the Soviet trade delegation when it took up residence in London.

Finally, Chicherin's Jewish comrades would have been surprised, to say the least, had they been given access to the transcript of a conversation he had with the Romanian Prince Bibesco who came to visit him in Brixton at the end of 1917, and to whom he confessed: 'I like very few Jews. Here my companions are a few murderers ...'

If Chicherin did his work among the Jewish revolutionaries and working men with distaste, he did not show it, at least not to Mrs Bridges Adams, whose admiration for him was complete. Writing shortly after he had gone back to Russia of the mission they had performed together in London, she recalled that '... he gave dignity and refinement to every piece of work he undertook for the worker's cause ... no words of mine can adequately describe [his] selfless devotion to the cause of his distressed compatriots in Russia and in Britain ...' Lord Sheffield, an old colleague of Mrs Bridges Adams from her days on the London Education Board, and Chicherin's mouthpiece in the House of Lords in the campaign to uphold the right of asylum, also described the future commissar as 'a man of honour and distinction'. And finally the editor of the *Observer* spoke of him as 'an accomplished gentleman, competent to hold his own among the diplomats of Europe'.

Among the various bodies that 'courted' the Russian Jews in Britain, it seems the Zionists were the least successful. In the summer of 1917, when the uncertainty about what to do was at its height, the community in London was visited by two interesting newcomers from Egypt, Vladimir Jabotinsky and Joseph Trumpeldor. When in 1914 the Turkish Ottoman Empire had offered Turkish citizenship to Jewish aliens in Palestine, 12,000 of them, including many Russian émigrés, had declined the invitation and were promptly deported to Egypt. Among them was Joseph Trumpeldor, who had lost an arm fighting for the Tsar, was decorated four times and commissioned in the field during the Russo-Japanese War, a rare, possibly unique, event for a Russian Jew. In Alexandria in 1915 he had met Vladimir Jabotinsky, a 35-year-old writer and journalist from Odessa who, like Trumpeldor, had become convinced that the Ottoman Empire, allied to the Central Powers, was doomed. As Zionists, they firmly believed that unless Jews were involved in the fighting to free Palestine from the Turks, they would have no claim to the redemption of Israel as the promised land of the Jewish people.

In March 1915 Jabotinsky and Trumpeldor had proposed to the British commander in Egypt, Lieutenant-General Sir John Maxwell, that a legion be formed of Jews who wished to fight against the Turks in Palestine. Maxwell turned them down on the grounds that an offensive in Palestine was unlikely, and because the British Army did not – yet – accept foreign nationals. He recommended instead that the volunteers form a mule transport unit for service in some other sector of the British front. Jabotinsky was offended by what seemed to him an ignominious suggestion, but Trumpeldor took the view that any anti-Turkish force would assist the Zionist cause and ultimately 'lead to Zion'. The Zion Mule Corps (ZMC) was duly formed under the command of Lieutenant-Colonel James Patterson, an Irish Protestant from Dublin, whose deep knowledge of the Old Testament inspired an interest in early Jewish history, and who would later, in British Mandate Palestine, come out as a firm ally of the Zionists. Meanwhile, 562 men of the Mule Corps were dispatched to Gallipoli, half of them allocated to the British and half to the Australians and New Zealanders (this half were unaccountably sent back to Egypt without seeing action). The 'British' half was at once flung into the Gallipoli bloodbath and, as the sole supply unit in operation, became an indispensable source of food, ammunition and other necessities, earning high praise from their commanders. By the end of the campaign only six of them had been killed and twenty-five wounded. The ZMC was disbanded a year later and its leading lights, Patterson, Jabotinsky and Trumpeldor, were sent to England.

The campaign to form a Jewish Legion for action in Palestine faced opposition from the British government and the War Office, which shared General Maxwell's misgivings and were not yet psychologically prepared to deal with the proposal. Another source of opposition came from such Jewish luminaries as Lord Rothschild and his circle who were unfriendly towards the Zionist idea in general. A third objection to a Jewish Legion came from the official Zionist leadership who had their own agenda to which they held doggedly. Jabotinsky would forever remain for them a thorn in the flesh, a militant who threatened to endanger their delicate diplomacy. And, of course, the idea of a Jewish regiment was noisily rebuffed by the majority of Russian Jews who were about to be sent back to Russia or forced to join the British Army.

Apart from Chicherin and the other Russian revolutionaries who were using the stalking-horse of the right of asylum to spread the idea of a workers' revolt, the Jewish workers of the East End had their own organisations, centred mostly on their trade unions, and they had their own political party, the General Jewish Workers' Union of Poland, Lithuania and Russia, which had been formed in Russia in 1897 as an integral part of the Russian Social Democratic Labour Party, and was known as the Bund ('union' in Yiddish). The Bund expressed the need for a nation-wide organisation in Russia to fight for the civil and political rights of the Jewish workers. As a socialist party, committed to the Russian Revolution and to the socialist future of the Jewish working class in Russia, it opposed the various Zionist solutions that envisaged mass resettlement. It also rejected the assimilationist solutions, which it regarded as impracticable for the Yiddish-speaking masses in Russia who had their own culture to develop. As the Jewish masses became more enlightened, the Bund predicted, they would throw off the blinkers of religious observance, and they would live as secular Jews, playing their part in Russia's socialist future. In many respects, this prediction was remarkably close to the eventual outcome.

By 1903 the Bund was claiming to represent all Jewish workers in the general party. When its claim was officially rejected by all the other delegates at the Russian Social Democratic Party congress – at which the party itself split into Bolsheviks and Mensheviks – the Bund went its separate way. More than the Russian party, the Bund presented a dual image – revolutionary organisation and trade union – a social institution that embraced the workplace, as well as the cultural life of the group. The organised life of Russian Jews, once they had settled in London, naturally tended to centre on everyday labour issues rather than political ones, while the Bund abroad had its true constituents back home in Russia, where its real political purpose lay. The war, and especially the threat of military service, brought these two separate concerns together. As Special Branch reported in April 1917, the Foreign Jews' Committee Against Repatriation and Compulsory Military Service embraced the Cap-Makers Union, the Industrial Workers of the World, the Bund, the British Socialist Party, as well as many individual members of the Yiddish Anarchist Federation and the 'Workers' Friend' Jewish Anarchist group.

A leading Bundist in London was Viktor Alter, an internationalist who, like Chicherin, arrived from Belgium at the outbreak of the war. After working for a while in a factory, Alter became closely involved in the Jewish trade unions and the British Socialist Party. In 1917 he addressed a mass meeting of English workers – 'an audience of three thousand cloth caps' – on the meaning of the February/March Revolution in Russia that had 'made the struggle against the war into a struggle for the revolution'. The line he took on conscription at this and similar meetings was indistinguishable from that of Chicherin.

By the eve of the war, as Menshevik policy on the national question virtually merged with that of the Bund, the two parties became allies, so that when a Menshevik delegation visited London, Paris and Rome in the summer of 1917, the Bund's leader in Russia, Henryk Erlikh, was one of its members. The delegation's purpose was to lobby socialist parties to attend or support the Stockholm Socialist Peace Conference, a noble enterprise that never took place. Like the majority of Mensheviks, Erlikh was a 'revolutionary defensist', advocating the defence of post-tsarist revolutionary Russia, while seeking every means to bring the war to an end in which no side would make territorial claims or reparations.*

The Menshevik delegates found themselves on the same ship as Arthur Henderson, a Labour member of Lloyd George's new War Cabinet who had been sent to Petrograd to replace Sir George Buchanan, the previous government's envoy. Henderson had sensibly recognised that he could not do a better job than Sir George and was now returning home. At first, the Mensheviks had given him the cold shoulder, regarding him as an advocate of 'war to a victorious conclusion', but they warmed to him when they realised his trip to Russia had fired him with an urge to support their efforts for peace and the resurrection of the Socialist International. But when they disembarked in London, to a welcome by the Labour Party, they were confronted by a delegation of Russian émigrés, led by an 'especially zealous' Chicherin, urging them not to compromise themselves by associating with a 'government party'. Chicherin told them that England was on the brink of revolution and that by accepting Labour's hospitality they would be cutting themselves off from the true revolutionary and internationalist elements of the English working class. Having just come from a city where revolutionary rhetoric of all colours was a round-the-clock feature of street life, the Mensheviks ignored Chicherin's warnings. They must also have known him as a man of wavering opinions.

In London, Erlikh addressed a meeting of Russian Jews in Yiddish about the condition of the Jews in Russia and the importance of the February/March Revolution for their future prospects. As the British press was under instruction from the Home Office to minimise publicity about the Convention and the impending return of Jews to Russia, only Erlikh's most anodyne remarks were reported, and only in the *Jewish Chronicle*. He warned those who were about to leave for Russia that, although they would

---

* Alter and Erlikh would be evacuated to the Soviet Union from Nazi-occupied Poland in 1940, ostensibly to head an Anti-Fascist Jewish Committee for the purpose of raising world Jewish support for the Soviet war effort. Instead, Erlikh committed suicide in a Kuibyshev prison, and Alter was executed there on 17 February 1943.

find life there 'full of interest', they must be prepared for great suffering, in view of the bad conditions and want of essentials – an understatement, if ever there was one.

5 The Convention

In Russian law, nationality was 'indelible'. All inhabitants of the Russian Empire, of whatever ethnic background, were Russian subjects. As a Jew, or as a 'Russian subject of the Jewish faith', one was deprived of some of the benefits of being a Russian subject, but never of the title itself, unless the sovereign himself chose so to do. Adoption of another citizenship did not automatically lead to loss of Russian nationality, even if it was done in contravention of Russian law, for example by leaving the country illegally to evade compulsory military service. Children born of Russian parents on British territory, and who under British law at the time were automatically British citizens, remained Russian subjects, at least in principle. In legal terms, then, it was correct to speak of the men subject to the Convention as 'Russians', even if what was understood was that they were Jews of Russian nationality.

As to whether the tsarist regime wanted its Jews to be sent back was answered by the Foreign Office in a memorandum: 'We know unofficially that the Russian government has no desire for the return of the Russian Jews to that country.' Russian policy on repatriation was meant to apply to what were termed 'real Russians', not Jews of Russian nationality. And these 'real' Russians would be handled by the Russian consul, whereas Russian Jews opting to return to Russia would be handled by the Metropolitan Police. This distinction was not novel to the Russian bureaucracy, which had plenty of practice in sorting out the non-Russian sheep of the empire from its Russian goats. In the mind of Russian officialdom, Russian Jews were aliens, not Russians, despite holding passports which clearly indicated that they were subjects of the Russian Empire.

The archives of the Imperial Russian Foreign Ministry contain countless files which show that 'real Russians' who refused military service were threatened with an eight-year prison sentence, though no mention was made of deprivation of citizenship. A hapless

Russian peasant who had somehow ended up in Denmark was pursued with futile relentlessness, and even Prince Kochubei, a descendant of Alexander I's illustrious friend, was bailed out of his debts by the Russian consul in Vancouver and threatened with gaol for evading military service. To the British official mind, it was official nationality that mattered, not ethnic affinity. The Russian government did not want these Jews back, and if they joined the British Army the British assumed there was a risk they would lose their Russian nationality. Since there was still no settled plan to offer British citizenship to friendly aliens in the British Army, Russian Jews in Britain were on their way to becoming stateless before the notion of statelessness existed.

In November 1916, the Russian consulate circulated a notice stating that Russians of military age must return at once to Russia and present themselves to the military authorities. The Foreign Office appeared unaware that the Russian authorities were going to great lengths to compel their exiles and émigrés to serve either in the Allied army where they happened to be, or to return to Russia where, if they failed to enlist, they would face penalties. It seems likely that unofficially this was known in Whitehall, as Sir George Buchanan was notified of growing unrest in the Jewish community in the East End: the threat of imprisonment for evasion in Russia must not appear in any Anglo-Russian agreement, but the terms of military service for Russians returning from Britain must be made clear.

The Russian draft agreement submitted in Petrograd stressed that Russians should return to Russia *as a first duty*, failing which they would be liable for service in the British Army. This was the exact opposite of the British government's approach, which kept repatriation, or deportation, as an ultimate sanction. The British government was convinced that the Russian Jews, believing that large-scale repatriation was not feasible, would apply to return in such large numbers as to make the scheme unworkable. Joseph King, who was thought by the Home Office to be acting 'no doubt on instructions', had already spoken of the shipping difficulties, and it was known that the Russian consulate was issuing visas and exemptions to increasing numbers of men claiming to want to go back, but secretly intending to go to America.

This practice was brought into the open at Bow Street magistrates court in December 1916, when four Russian Jews, all bachelors in their mid-twenties, two diamond-cutters and two tailors, were charged under the Defence of the Realm Act with making false statements to the Russian consulate in order to obtain passports to Russia. It transpired that the Vice-Consul, Ernest Gambs, had issued the passports despite, as he admitted in court, not believing that the men had any intention of returning to Russia, still less of serving in the army, as they had professed. He had even noted his doubts in the passports themselves, adding 'and then we leave it to the authorities', in other words, leaving it to the discretion of the Metropolitan Police whether to pass or detain the passport-holder. The case against the men was that they had been found on a Danish ship en route from Christiania (Oslo) in Norway to New York when, as was routine in wartime, she was stopped by a British naval vessel and escorted into Kirkwall in the Orkney Islands. There she was searched for war contraband by the Admiralty port officer, accompanied by a Metropolitan Police inspector. The four defendants had been found in possession of passports obtained fraudulently, and after four days detention in Edinburgh Castle were brought to Bow Street. The magistrate decided he had no jurisdiction in the matter, granted bail and applied for a ruling by the High Court, where it was in turn referred to the Lord Chief Justice and the Attorney General.

The defence's argument was that, having been forcibly removed from a neutral ship on the high seas, the defendants had been brought to Britain by an illegal act and it was therefore wrong to detain them. Furthermore, the Danish ship had entered Kirkwall under potential duress, for had the captain not cooperated his ship would have been seized under international law. It also argued that whether the passports were acquired legally or fraudulently was irrelevant, since an act offensive to the state had not been committed by their acquisition. The court, which knew precisely who it was dealing with, was indifferent to the police inspector's testimony that, when he asked the defendants what their nationality was, one of them replied, 'Internationals'.*

The judgment of the court was that the arrests had been properly made and that, since neither the Danish nor Russian governments had complained, no international law had been broken. As for the main charge, the men had given as their reason for wanting passports their desire to return to Russia to fight, that is, indirectly to help the British war effort. Their offence therefore *was* relevant to

---

* In the spring of 1917 Trotsky was detained in similar circumstances and responded to the same question, 'Social Democrat'.

the country's wartime interests. The Lord Chief Justice upheld the magistrate's ruling and the men were remanded pending a final appeal against deportation. A pamphlet containing the main evidence and judgments was immediately published, together with a letter from Lord Sheffield campaigning for funds.

The Liberal and left-wing press was predictably indignant. With the aim of undermining the scheme to deport men back to Russia for military service, the *Manchester Guardian* defended the principle that the government did not have the right to tell a deported alien where he must go: 'A deported alien can go to any country he pleases.' The anti-war, internationalist weekly *The Call* announced melodramatically: 'The case of the four Russian Jews must not be allowed to create a precedent for an act which, if perpetrated, would be one of the greatest crimes committed during the war.' In fact, the Court of Appeal agreed with the defence that no crime had been committed and the case was dropped.

The British government which was still committed to enlisting aliens into the British Army as a first choice, was also determined to satisfy the Russian government that proper form was being observed, and remained committed to the notion that if the Russian consul issued travel documents to Scandinavia, or exemptions according to Russian regulations, these would be honoured by the British authorities. Knowing that the Russian consul was issuing travel documents to applicants who had no intention of returning to Russia, the British inserted an amendment into the draft agreement allowing men to apply for exemption on the grounds of wanting to serve in Russia, adding that the Russian consulate should be responsible for handling such applications.

As a further means of putting pressure on those who were likely to apply to return to Russia, a clause was inserted requiring that 'they shall pay their own travelling expenses', perhaps one of the most unrealistic proposals in the negotiations, even if the fare from Liverpool to Archangel in the north of Russia would turn out to be no more than £8, which still amounted to average wages for three or four weeks. The last clause of the Russian draft stipulated that the agreement would lose force on the day peace was signed, there being no reason at that date to suppose that all the Allies would not make peace at the same time – a reckless opinion, as it would turn out. Finally, the draft stated that, the war over, men in Allied armies would be entitled to be sent back to the place where they were called up. For Russian Jews from England, that plainly meant England. The Foreign Office deleted this clause, taking the view that 'if Russian Jews opted not to serve here but to go back to Russia, then they would have to stay there after the war, and not expect to be able to return here as though nothing had happened'.

By the time the question was raised again in parliament, Russia was no longer ruled by a tsar; she had a new – Provisional – government. How this liberal institution would deal with the question of recruiting a few thousand Russian subjects abroad was yet to be seen. The British government was deeply relieved at the news of the February/March Revolution. Nicholas II had plainly lost his prestige and the support of the people, his administration had been exposed as ineffectual, and it was hoped in Britain, as it was in Russia, that the men in the Provisional government would translate their criticism of the old regime into an effective war effort. The fact that the Provisional government was also committed to profound democratic reform was an added bonus, for now the United States need feel no moral compunction about entering the war on Russia's side. At the prompting of the Russian chargé d'affaires, the British government sent a cable to the new premier, Prince Lvov, who despite his title was a committed democrat, declaring their satisfaction at the turn of events and granting immediate recognition to the new government in Petrograd.*

With tsarism gone and a democratically minded government installed, one of whose first acts had been formally to abolish the Pale of Jewish Settlement and announce universal civil equality, the Anglo-Russian negotiations on military service for the Russian Jews in Britain gathered pace. The Russian military representative in London, General Desino, urged his government that further delay was politically undesirable. 'The British government should settle the issue by offering Russian Jews in England a choice of either going back to Russia or joining the British Army, whether it be in special units or like everyone else.' A draft was ready by late May.

While Joseph King called on the government to facilitate the return of many Russians who were 'anxious to return to Russia forthwith ... to fight for their native soil', and the Metropolitan Police took the jaundiced view that neither the Jews nor the Russians who had been applying in large numbers to the Russian consulate had the slightest

---

* The Germanic name of St Petersburg had been russified at the outbreak of war.

intention of going anywhere near an army once they were back in Russia, negotiations stalled. Since the idea of deportation dominated the debate, it is surprising to find the Foreign Office stating unequivocally that 'the idea of deportation has long been abandoned, and is indeed impracticable owing to tonnage difficulties; in any case the scheme produced little or no result, and the regulations have no bearing on the present situation'. The British held to their view that entry into the British Army should take precedence, and return to Russia the second choice. To give the appearance of reciprocity, a clause was included under which British men of military age in Russia would have to exercise a similar choice – join the Russian Army or return to Britain. But it had already been made clear in Buchanan's correspondence with the Foreign Office that Britons should not be conscripted into the Russian Army because the conditions were too harsh. They should instead be able to return to the United Kingdom via Scandinavia. In July Buchanan would inform the government that the total number of British men of military age who had wives and families in Russia amounted to 500.

At an inter-departmental conference, held on 5 June 1917, the Admiralty objected strongly to providing any transport; it was already cutting convoys to a minimum and was therefore dead against shipping Russians from Britain to Archangel. This came as a shock to the Foreign Office which had already informed the Russian government that Britain was prepared to transport 20,000 men before ice closed the route, and assumed the Russians had based their proposals on this information. The Admiralty eventually conceded that it might handle 6,000 men, as long as they all sailed in one group of ships. The question now was whether the Russian government would accept these terms and whether the agreement would be workable if more than 6,000 decided to go back.

The British were uneasy about sending large numbers of interned anarchists and pro-German agitators to Russia where they could work against the Russian war effort. But it also believed that the Russian government was determined to carry out the scheme, and therefore the problem of transporting large numbers had to be faced. Imprisoned or interned revolutionaries should be considered outside the agreement, unless the Russian government – which was after all a 'revolutionary government' – specifically asked for their return. The British view was that it would be best left unmentioned to avoid trouble. As for the Russian consul's practice of dishing out certificates freely, the Russian authorities would have to be trusted 'to play fair'.

The most difficult aspect of the agreement was its practicality. According to Buchanan, the Russian Provisional government did not like the idea that its citizens in Britain could be conscripted into the British Army without first being given the choice of going back to Russia, and it had asked the British to determine how many men would choose to return. The Home Office, wishing to avoid any hint of a 'round-up', had decided not to conduct a proper survey, and had asked the Metropolitan Police Commissioner for a rough estimate. He replied that scarcely 100 men would opt to go back, adding that the Foreign Office's figure of 20,000 should not be made public, as it might provoke a mass application from men trying to sabotage the system by overloading it.

The inter-departmental conference concluded that shipping space for even as few as 6,000 would not be needed in the end, though this would not be made known to the Russian government, which was only concerned that men should be able to return if they wanted to. The Admiralty, regarding the initiative as an unwanted extra burden on its resources, threw a last minute spanner into the works by insisting that Russians who opted to return be sent to fight in France instead of Russia, as this would make it possible to close the U-boat-infested Archangel route altogether. Others countered by pointing out that the Russian government was insisting on the option to return and any sabotage of that option would only lead to the collapse of the scheme, arguing that 'if the Russian Jews had wanted to go to fight in France, they would have signed up for the British Army in the first place!'

The general consensus was that it was best to accept the Russian draft without mentioning either the amount of space available or the idea of sending the men to France. In view of the small numbers likely to be involved, it was also agreed to pay the transport costs, as the Russians had requested. The meeting realised that the scheme could be defeated by an excessive flood of applications to return, but it felt there was no alternative but to face the risk. If the scheme were to break down altogether, it would cause unrest in the East End and embarrass the Foreign Office in its relations with Russia.

According to the Metropolitan Police, whose information on the situation, though imperfect, was the best available, the Russian Jews would do anything to gain time, short of coming out in the open and holding public meetings: 'This they would not do on account of the strength of the feeling against them, not only on the part of the English, but also of British-born and other Jews, many of whom had lost sons at the Front. These feel very bitter against the Russian Jews, and the extraordinary position they have taken up. The present hope of the Russian Jews is to get postponement for six months, when they hope the War may be over.' The police report went on: 'The idea that they will return to Russia if facilities are given is pure bluff. A very large number of them came over in infancy, and speak no language but English, and a few words of Yiddish. Their relations are all settled in this country, and they would far rather go into the British Army if they are compelled, than return with a free passage.' Although some of this was true, the material point, about preferring to join the British Army to going back to Russia, would soon be shown to be flawed.

The Russian Imperial ambassador, Count Alexander Benckendorff, died in January 1917, and before the tsarist government had time to appoint his successor it became defunct itself. The Counsellor, Constantine Nabokov, was left in charge. His brother was Vladimir Nabokov (father of the writer), a leading liberal and now the head of the Provisional government's secretariat. Since the embassy remained technically an agency of the old regime, Constantine found his position made difficult by the fact that he did not hide his joy at the overthrow of the Romanov dynasty. Colleagues regarded his behaviour as dishonourable and he was ostracised.

Divisions also existed within the British government. Senior officials who were sceptical about the revolution and feared that it might fatally weaken Russia as a military power judged the new government purely in terms of how well or badly it was likely to continue fighting. The Foreign Office disapproved of Nabokov and expected a new ambassador to arrive. With extraordinary lack of judgment, imagining that a known imperialist would suit the London scene, the Provisional government appointed a former ambassador and recent tsarist foreign minister, Sergei Sazonov. Dropped within a few weeks, Sazonov left Nabokov in charge. During the Civil War he would represent Admiral Alexander Kolchak's White government at the Paris Peace Conference.

In his memoirs, Nabokov recalled that the Russian colony in London consisted of two distinct groups. The first included embassy personnel, military, naval, financial and other permanent officers of the Russian government, plus government officials who were in London in connection with the war effort, all amounting to about 500 people. Most of them were monarchist, if not outright reactionary, in their political views. The fact that many of them swore allegiance to the Provisional government 'with their fingers crossed behind their backs' was not admired by British officials, and this complicated relations between the two governments.

The other group consisted of the 1,000 or so political émigrés, refugees from the secret police, and they of course were all for the new regime, at least for the time being. They despised the embassy and viewed it with the suspicion of fugitives from the regime it had represented. Before the February/March Revolution the embassy naturally had no relations with this part of the Russian community, except when some essential service, such as the issue of a passport, was required. The Revolution changed all that, and now it was the embassy's job as far as possible to reconcile and guide Russian circles in Britain, as well as to establish and develop relations on a new basis with the British government, the press and public opinion.

The very first instruction Nabokov received from the new foreign ministry in Petrograd, headed now by the liberal professor of history, Paul Milyukov, was to take the necessary steps to organise the repatriation of all Russians who had fled abroad. The task of forming an émigré committee proved simple, as the émigrés themselves made the first approach, when two representatives turned up at the embassy – Kruglyakov and Chicherin. Organising the repatriation itself turned out to be more difficult. Although London had become the centre to which Russians had flocked when the Continent was cut off from Russia by the war, in spring 1917 the Germans chose to launch their so-called sink without trace (*spurlos versenkt*) policy in the North Sea.

Ostensibly, the British government did not wish to place obstacles in the path of Russians wishing to return home. But many émigrés were married and domiciled in Britain, and the question arose whether those applying to return should also be compelled to take their families with them. On the other hand, to insist on this would virtually amount to blocking their departure, since women and children were not allowed to travel on British naval ships, and very few other ships were available. The government had no desire to alienate its Russian ally by taking any harsh action towards Russian citizens and was reminded by the Home Office that, 'The result would be the detention in this country of a somewhat undesirable class and the risk of creating an unfavourable impression in Russia that the British authorities were obstructing the return of men in sympathy with the revolution.' The Provisional government made clear its wish to repatriate the *political* émigrés by allocating two million roubles to the Foreign Ministry for this purpose, leaving the Jewish refugees out of the reckoning. Meanwhile, as many as 2,500 Russian subjects of all stripes, including Jews, were given visas by the Russian consulate during the summer.

* * *

The Russian Army was arguably the single most revolutionary factor at work in the Russia of 1917. Its behaviour, command staff and rank and file were all essential components in the political history of the period until the end of the Civil War. And the Russian Army in 1917 was in a state of mounting turmoil and disarray. Even Russian contingents that had been sent to support the Allies in France were quickly infected by the revolutionary fever that was rampant back home.

In 1916, the Tsar had responded positively to a request from the French to send two large brigades of troops to assist on the Western Front. (Two further brigades were shipped via France to fight on the Macedonian Front.) The Russian brigades (1st and 3rd) were made up largely of peasants from the Volga region and workers from the Moscow area. The latter included many veterans of the 1905 Revolution and labour organisations, and even illegal revolutionary groups. Some of them might well have been sent to France by commanding officers eager to get rid of agitators, and French police agents duly spotted some of them in contact with Russian revolutionaries in Paris. In the cafés, on leave, worker-soldiers listened to their loquacious comrades discussing the iniquity of the war, and were only too willing to believe that they had been sent as cannon-fodder in exchange for French arms. In the terrible winter of 1916, alongside the French, the Russian units suffered severe losses. Morale sank, followed by unrest in the Russian camp. Severe punishment was meted out, a provocation by the commandant backfired, a colonel was stoned to death and eight men were executed by firing squad.

Then came the fall of the Tsar. An address to the Russian troops serving with Allied armies was published in Paris by the Russian Social Democratic Party in April 1917, describing in detail the 'democratisation' of the army that had taken place at home. The most important change was that soldiers' soviets (councils) were vetting all orders to ensure they conformed to the Petrograd Soviet's 'defence policy', namely, that the army must engage only in defensive acts. The message underlying the words of the address was that the line of command had been turned upside down and the Russian Army was fast becoming ungovernable. The address called on the men abroad to honour their fallen comrades by tying red banners to their company colours.

Within weeks the brigades were forming soviets of their own and demanding immediate repatriation. Instead they were persuaded to swear an oath of allegiance to the Provisional government and in April 1917 they returned to the front to fight alongside the French at Rheims. But the battle was both bloody and futile and the Russians lost 3,000 men out of their total of 19,000. Pulled back from the front, they were in a state of near anarchy, 10,000 men laid down their arms and mounted mass demonstrations demanding repatriation. Only 6,000 remained loyal to their oath. Bolshevik-inspired in all but name, defeatist agitation and propaganda spread rapidly. On 1 May the men staged a mass rally and a revolutionary parade, openly insulting their commander, General Palitsyn, and jeering him to an ignominious retreat when, mounted on his white charger, he tried to address them. The deterioration of the Russian brigades now accelerated. Inflamed by the oratory of a few competent agitators, the troops insulted and attacked their officers and flagrantly ignored orders.

Meanwhile, as the French continued to suffer heavy losses in futile operations, the 'Russian virus' took hold among them, too, leading to many courts martial and executions, though apparently not enough to halt the progress of the disease. In the summer of 1917, the Russian Provisional government came out in support of an international peace conference to be held in Stockholm, giving the Western Allies good reason to fear that Russia would leave the war early, abandoning them to face increased German strength. The French Commander-in-Chief, General Philippe Pétain, recognizing the new political circumstances, remarked that 'the danger of 75 German divisions attacking us is much less than the demoralisation of our armies'.

It was decided in June that the Russians must be isolated. An army camp at La Courtine on the barren moors of the Massif Central, containing thousands of troops and German prisoners of war, was cleared in ten days and the Russian 3rd Brigade was put there, surprisingly still equipped with automatic weapons, light artillery and ammunition. The change of location did nothing to lighten their mood. Homesickness became more gnawing, exacerbated by the scarcity of the mail from Russia. An outright mutiny was brewing. Some officers tried to reason with their men, reminding them that their homeland had been invaded by the Germans. They replied: 'What's that to us? Doesn't Russia have a lot of land? There's enough for the whole world! And what good's liberty to me if I'm dead?' Meanwhile, in July the 6,000 men of 1st Brigade, who were mostly peasants, arrived at La Courtine, and at once there was friction between the revolutionary-minded 3rd Brigade and the new arrivals. By August, the intimidated peasants of 1st Brigade decided enough was enough, and of their own accord moved out of La Courtine and set up camp at Felletin, 17 miles away.

At La Courtine the mayhem worsened. In July the French War Ministry urged the Provisional government to have all 16,000 men shipped back to Russia, but there was no shipping to be had from any of the Allies – and this at a time when the British government was telling the Russian government that 20,000 Russian Jews could be shipped back to Russia. On 1 August General Zankevich issued an ultimatum to the men at La Courtine to surrender their arms and themselves within forty-eight hours or face punishment as traitors. Six weeks later the rebels were still refusing all mediation and demanding that only repatriation would satisfy them. On 14 September, the 3,000 'loyalists' of 3rd Brigade joined the 2nd Russian Artillery Brigade and French supporting forces and surrounded the camp. The rebels were given two days. At 10 a.m. on the 16th the 75mm guns fired warning shots. Inside the camp, the rebels thought the siege was a bluff. But in the afternoon the bombardment was real enough, though the gunners were under orders to avoid casualties, if possible. Next day the shelling was still heavier and the men gave up. The authorities reported nine dead.

While the ringleaders were sent to a prison island, the rest were kept La Courtine. The French government would have been happy to send them home to Russia, but with the Provisional government facing internal and external crises, Prime Minister Alexander Kerensky had no stomach for another 10,000 riotous troops in the capital, and told the French he preferred the shipping to be used to bring arms to Russia instead.

To resolve the problem themselves, the French chose to disperse the men, offering them paid work in factories, farming, forestry or military installations. About 9,600 accepted, leaving 4,330 hard cases to suffer internment in North Africa. The men were also offered the chance to fight the Germans again, this time in a Legion of Russian Volunteers. About 300 of the mutineers chose this path, some of them, as they wrote home, in order to restore the good name of revolutionary Russia which had been 'dishonoured by our local maximalists', others 'to regain the personal dignity which those who chose manual labour would not have'.

The majority, meanwhile, simply waited for the day when the French and Russian governments could agree on their repatriation, their minds full of dreams of the socialist paradise they were missing in Russia, compared to which France now appeared as the ungrateful heart of capitalism. They in turn were seen by the French as traitors to the cause of freedom and democracy, especially after the Treaty of Brest-Litovsk in March 1918. They would be greeted in the street with cries of '*Cochons!*' and '*Boches!*' French intelligence at Dieppe suggested that an increase in the mail from Russia would be beneficial, as it would show these dreamers what was really happening at home. The flow did increase, but so did the homesickness and the hatred for France. When the armistice was finally signed in November 1918, the Russian soldiers were told that members of the Russian Volunteers Legion, having taken part in the final offensive, would get home first. Many signed on, but very few of them intended fighting the Bolsheviks. One wrote home: 'I'm sure that if they take us back to Russia, there'll be very few left in the Legion, everyone will scatter in all directions, very few are sincere, most have been infected by Bolshevism.'

Meanwhile, the presence of large numbers of Russian soldiers on the French Riviera did little to further the cordiality of the Entente. Since April 1917 Russian troops had been refusing to embark for Salonika on the Balkan front, ostensibly because the order had not been ratified by the Russian government. Their public behaviour was universally deplored, nowhere more so than by the good citizens of La Seyne sur Mer. In November 'a group of Fathers and Mothers of sons at the front' wrote to the war minister to request that the Russians be removed from the village which was being asked to house 'these traitors who ought to have been put into a concentration camp long ago'. The Russians caused disorderly scenes, 'paid for with German

gold', and the community was affronted by the continued Russian
occupation of a splendid school 'whose many pupils have shown their
patriotism and given their lives for France'. By November the Russian
troops at Hyères were in a state of total anarchy. They were still
refusing to embark for Salonika and the French warned them that two
companies of Senegalese troops would be deployed to 'encourage'
them. The threat was enough to ensure embarkation without incident
on 15 December 1917. One can only surmise that, like the men of the
Russian Legion, these troops were agreeing to embark with the
intention of staying well clear of any fighting.

* * *

It was against this background of refusal, revolutionary agitation,
protest and disintegration of the Russian Army that the British
government set about implementing the Anglo-Russian Military
Service Convention in the summer of 1917. The Russian war
ministry still regarded the army as a viable entity with an unremit-
ting need for new recruits. Even as late as 22 October 1917, only
days before the Bolshevik seizure of power, it was still applying the
rules. When the Petrograd Soviet asked the war ministry what its
position was on Russian citizens returning to Russia for military
service, the ministry explained that bona fide 'politicals' would have
forty days' grace to organise their affairs before enlistment, but non-
political emigrants who were arriving in Russia and who had applied
to serve in the Russian Army for the duration of the war, were
subject to immediate call-up. The Russian authorities were
determined that the Convention should not be seen or used as a way
of evading military service. At Nabokov's prompting, on 21 August
Kerensky, who was both prime minister and war minister, released
an announcement to the British press telling those about to return to
Russia that they 'would be given an immediate opportunity to fulfil
their military duty ... Upon their arrival in Russia, they will be
enlisted, equipped, and distributed to training centres'.

The British government was undertaking commitments in the
belief that it would not have to carry them out; the Russian government had the authority to accomplish its declared intentions, but as
summer faded into autumn its power to do anything was draining
away. Nevertheless, the Military Service (Conventions with Allied
States) Act, 1917, was enacted in July. Russian males of military age
who wished to return to Russia were given twenty-one days from 19

July to apply to their local police station. No application could be made after 9 August and applications made before that date could not be withdrawn after it. Those who chose to return were to be ready to go at any time after 13 August. Failure to sail after receiving notice would render the delinquent liable to military service in Britain, without the right of appeal for exemption. The government could give no undertaking about repatriating wives and children with men who opted to go back. No separation allowances were envisaged: Conventionists would have to make their own arrangements for the maintenance of their families in their absence.

Any Russian who did not opt to return would be liable for military service like other citizens, but would have until 19 September to apply for exemption. Once enlisted in the British Army they would have the same rights and privileges as British subjects in terms of pay, pension, separation allowances and so on, and they would be granted British naturalisation without fee after three months' service, if they applied to the Home Office and could satisfy the statutory conditions. Any Russian who had registered for service in the British Army, but had not yet been enlisted, was entitled to apply to return to Russia. Finally, the Convention did not apply to Russians who were already serving in the British Army.

A question remained over Russians who were working in British munitions factories. It was assumed that after 10 August they would come under the Military Service Acts and that their call-up would be regulated on the same basis as British munitions workers. According to MI5, there were 2,400 Russians working on munitions. Of them, fewer than 600 held certificates from the Russian consul stating that the Russian government had no objection to their being engaged on such work, and 100 had certificates saying that Russian law permitted the deferment of military service while a man was working on munitions. MI5 did not think that many more than these numbers would turn out to be on war work, 'as the bulk of applicants [for such certificates] seem to be tailors'. But, clearly unknown to MI5, the labour authorities had been granting exemption to men who were engaged in factories making army uniforms, a large number of them Russian Jews. Competition for such jobs among men threatened with deportation was naturally fierce, but the factories could only employ so many.

On 8 August, as the deadline approached, Scotland Yard reported to the Home Office that some 2,500 Russian Jews had already applied to return to Russia and many more were applying. The police believed that most of the applicants had no intention of actually going back, but were simply responding to agitators who were telling them that if enough applied the government would be unable to cope through lack of shipping. There were also those who ignored Kerensky's assurances and thought that even if they did go they would not have to serve. Up to 8 August 100 Russians had been given notice about arrangements for their departure, and the police were keen to ensure that nothing should disrupt their plans. The Russian Jews must understand that the choice was a real one: either serve here or go back to Russia. Any further delay would only strengthen the agitators' arguments.

Although the police were convinced the Russian Jews were waiting until the last moment before applying, and would then pack the police stations and cause mayhem, Scotland Yard assured the Home Secretary that they would cope. The authorities had agreed in principle to pay the rail fares of returnees, but even at this late date no arrangements had been made. The police did not think they could insist on prepayment and, with an uncharacteristic failure of imagination, suggested that 'the passengers', as these deportees were now described, should be charged at the point of embarkation, if they happened to have any money in their possession.

Nor must medical examinations be allowed to cause delay, though the British authorities and the Russian embassy responded to protests by establishing a system of sorts to ensure that men who applied either to return or for exemption were properly examined. The late Dr Samuel Sacks, a Russian Jew himself, and father of the well-known neurologist Oliver Sacks, told me his first job, as a newly qualified houseman at the London Hospital in the East End, had been to examine Russians who were returning to Russia. He also remembered that one of his colleagues, another Russian Jew, was dismissed for handing out exemption certificates too readily. Still, there were Conventionists who were irritated by the fact that they were *not* being medically examined before embarking. The *Jewish Chronicle*, which was otherwise not well disposed towards departing Jews, commented: 'A man may abandon his business, leave his family and travel a considerable distance in dangerous seas, only to be [medically] rejected upon arrival in Russia.' The authorities in Swansea, at least, were following correct procedure: Harris Levine, a draper in that city, passed a medical, but his two brothers failed. Whether or not men went through medical examination, the whole scheme was plainly carried out with minimum preparation, as though the authorities wanted to be rid of an embarrassment.

In mid-October, the Home Office reported that 7,600 men had applied to return under the scheme. The following sailings had taken place: in the *Pollern* which left on 15 August, out of 52 who had been expected 45 had gone; on 31 August the *Bienvenue* departed with 94 men, 17 having failed to show. On 10 September the largest contingent of 1,700 men had embarked in two ships, the *Kursk* and the *Stenkov*, 1,300 having failed to show. Then, on 19 September the *Umgeni* had set out with 56 men, but the ship was damaged, probably by a torpedo, though this was not disclosed, had turned back and her passengers were now waiting for another transport. On 29 September the *Tsaritsa* had left Hull with about 200 men. On 30 September the *Porto*, with 1,050 men out of 2,600 who had been notified, was also damaged some way out and returned with the men who were now waiting in a camp somewhere in Lancashire. In round figures, this meant that about 3,145 men had embarked out of 7,600 who had been expected. The shipments had begun quietly, even surreptitiously. Given that the total number of men who may have been liable was 31,500, and that 4,000 had opted to join the British Army, a rate of 23 per cent meant that from the government's point of view the scheme was clearly a failure.

6 The Journey

The first opportunity to send men to Russia under the Convention came less than a week after the deadline, on 15 August, when a British ship, the *Pollern* leaving Liverpool, was authorised to carry 52 men who had applied under the Act. The ship was also carrying political exiles and their families, as well as some Russian pilots who had been training in Britain. Little contact was made between these very different categories of passenger, the pilots as haughtily disdainful of their Jewish 'compatriots' as they were of the 'politicals'. The departure of such a small group, at a time when ships carrying Russians home were leaving British ports and arriving fairly regularly, attracted no attention. Nor was it meant to: the Home Office was so concerned that 'if any of them are sunk, there will be trouble', it had ordered Special Branch to instruct the press censors not to allow any reference to Russians leaving Britain for service in the Russian Army.*

On the day of the first departure, the Home Office informed the Ministry of Shipping that the total number of men who had registered a desire to return was now 7,500, of whom 5,000 were in London, 1,000 in Lanarkshire and 500 in Glasgow, the remaining 1,000 being scattered among other cities. Although no one was under any illusion that all those who had registered would in fact turn up, the time had come for a final effort to carry out the Convention. In the first week of September, the police undertook one last sweep of the billiard halls, restaurants and clubs of the East End. Among the survivors whom I interviewed, a shared memory was of being stopped on the street by policemen on a sunny Saturday afternoon and reminded of their now unavoidable responsibilities.

---

* Nor was coverage given to the extraction of British subjects from Russia by naval ships at that time; these were the families (many of them Anglo-Russian) of the engineers and sales and managerial staff of companies that had contributed significantly to the industrialisation of Russia since the mid-nineteenth century.

On 10 September the Metropolitan Police escorted a long procession from the East End, joined by a smaller one, including the brothers Shukman from the West End, and marshalled them at King's Cross Station. There, in torrential rain, a large crowd, variously estimated at between 2,000 and 5,000 people, which had assembled to see the men off, had to be kept out by police to clear a way for the voyagers. Flora Benenson Solomon described the 'miserable, perplexed picture' of the first stage of the journey back to 'their hated homeland ... There were only about a thousand altogether, for many must have been lying low, or were able, by some ingenuity, to postpone the day. Clutching sandwiches wrapped in newspaper and their cardboard suitcases, these men had the lost look of a crowd unable to move except where directed. But while some wept, others looked relieved, and joked among themselves. Wives had to remain behind ... Some of these women would never see their husbands again.'

There were in fact 609 men, and this was the largest company of Conventionists to leave London. Similar, smaller groups were leaving Manchester, Leeds, Cardiff and Glasgow at the same time, all converging on Liverpool where they would embark in the Russian ships *Kursk* and *Stenkov* for the voyage across the North Sea, around the top of Norway to the northern Russian port of Archangel. Most of the passenger traffic from northern Russia before the war had been carried from the Baltic port of Libau (Libava) by ships of the Russian East Asian Steamship Company. This was the Russian branch of the Jewish Colonisation Society, a joint-stock company which, among other things, organised the emigration of Jews, as well as other ethnic groups from Poland and the Baltic provinces, chiefly to America. It had been evacuated from Libau in the early weeks of the war and was now engaged on the Arctic route.

No doubt emotions at King's Cross were mixed. Many of these men had never expected that their obduracy would lead to this. Sharing workshops, living in neighbouring flats and rooms, meeting constantly at their social centres, in their clubs, pubs and teashops and on street corners, they had spent months on end arguing and agonising over what to do. Many had made themselves scarce by getting away to Ireland, where there was no conscription, or to small towns on the south coast, while others had succeeded where the famous 'Four Russian Jews' had failed and gone to America. Among those remaining, many had changed their minds as many as three times in the weeks before the deadline, signing on and signing off, and some changed their minds on the very day and went into hiding or went off to join the British Army. It had been commonly believed, and hoped, that that they would cause the system to break down through overload; or that it would be too difficult to send each man to his hometown in Russia where, as they thought, they would have to go to be inducted into the Russian Army; or that it would take so many months to find the shipping that the war would long be over. But all these possibilities evaporated as they waited to board trains that would take them to Liverpool and a worryingly uncertain future.

The perplexity observed by Flora Solomon was understandable. The married men had left their families – with 1,700 children in London alone – to fend for themselves. Not until after July 1918 would the government allocate funds for maintenance, but only 500 women are recorded as receiving support in 1920. Despite the fact that many of the women were skilled in the customary trades of tailoring and dressmaking, their immediate future looked bleak, and their men knew it.

Then, there was the very real fear of the hazardous journey facing the Conventionists, the North Sea being infested with German U-boats, and there was also the lurking doubt that military service in Russia might, despite the revolutionary chaos there, still be required of them. And, as no one had yet raised the question whether they would be allowed to return to Britain after the war was over, they must have wondered if they would ever join their wives and families again. They were after all aliens with virtually no rights, they had systematically resisted the moral pressure of public opinion and the official pressure of a friendly government, and they had taken the riskiest step any alien who wishes to retain the right of abode can take – they were leaving the country.

They may have looked like a flock of sheep, but every man had his own thoughts. Whereas family men may have feared they had made a mistake, leaving their wives and children in a London that had become used to take shelter from German bombs in the Underground, many of the single men were only too eager to join the Revolution, and saw the Convention as a chance to take part in a great adventure, to assist at the birth of a new society, to engage in class war rather than the carnage of world war. The night before their departure there were loud farewell parties, with revolutionary songs to celebrate the event. Some men were leaving to escape from

1. David Shukman, the author's father, after his return to London in 1920, the photograph bears part of the stamp of the Russian Consulate in London

2. Masha Shukman, either when leaving Russia in 1913 or c.1920 after David Shukman's return

3. Israel Shukman (Sugarman), the author's uncle, who returned to Russia with David Shukman a few years after the photo was taken

4. David Shukman's aliens registration book

5. Herbert Samuel, reproduced courtesy
Parliamentary Archives, SAM/C

6. Poster for a meeting in London,
January 1918

7. The arrival of the SS *Tsaritsa*, Archangel, summer 1917

8. Postcard of Archangel, reproduced courtesy John Massey-Stewart

9. Postcard of Vologda, a provincial town in central Russia, reproduced courtesy John Massey-Stewart

10. Litvinov (left) and Chicherin (right), at the Geneva Conference, 1922

11. Lenin, Moscow, 1918, Stalin is in the background on the right

12. May Day, Moscow, 1919

13. Postcard of Chelyabinsk station on the Trans-Siberian Railway, reproduced courtesy John Massey-Stewart

14. Postcard of part of the port system at Vladivostok, reproduced courtesy John Massey-Stewart

15. Postcard of Sebastopol, reproduced courtesy John Massey-Stewart

16. Interior Ministry permit for David Shukman to reside in Moscow for seven days, October 1917

To whom it may concern.

This is to certify that No.234b David Sugarman is a civilian attached to the Black Sea Labour Corps, and is employed as a tailor at the Army Training Schools, Constantinople.

MASLAK.   Capt. & Adjutant.
17-6-1919.

OD.

This is to certify that David Sugerman has been employed at these Schools as a Tailor from 1st May, 1919 to 3rd Sept, 1919.

He has done excellent work and is very trustworthy. I am very sorry to loose him.

Constantinople.   Capt. for
3-9-1919   Lieut-Colonel, Commandant,
                          Army Training Schools.

17a/b. Two British Military Mission documents given to David Shukman in Constantinople which enabled him to get back into Britain

an unhappy marriage, others were going with the eager encouragement of an unhappy wife. Hinde Esther Kreitman, sister of the
famous Yiddish writer Isaac Bashevis Singer, and herself a writer,
had fled to London from Belgium when the Germans invaded, and
when her husband Abraham went back to Russia as a Conventionist
she was glad to see the back of him. Others seized the opportunity
to see the families they had left behind in Russia. But they must all
have shared the feeling that though they were taking a leap into the
unknown, somehow they would find a way back to the lives they
were leaving behind. Escorted by police officers from Scotland Yard,
they made the overnight journey to Liverpool in damp discomfort,
embarked next morning on the *Kursk* and *Stenkov* and headed for
northern waters.

There was a certain irony in the fact that, as the convoy was leaving
British waters, a French freighter, the *Melbourne*, was landing about
300 Russian troops at Invergordon, in Scotland. Aware that the
British public was hostile to the calls for an immediate peace coming
from Russia, the Russian troops disembarked unsure of their reception. To their relief, they found themselves being led in formation by
a pipe band through the town to the railway station, where they
boarded the train for the journey through England, around London
to Folkestone, across the Channel, through France to Marseilles and,
vainly as it turned out, onward by ship to the front at Salonika. They
had been raised as a volunteer brigade by Count Nikolai Lobanov-
Rostovsky and, together with 150 French civilians from Romania and
an order of Catholic nuns, had embarked at Archangel at the
beginning of September, surreptitiously like the Conventionists, but
for the opposite reason of the anti-war mood in Russia.

Almost as soon as the *Kursk* convoy left Liverpool, some of the
men experienced new doubts about the decision to go, and even
approached the ship's officers to ask if it was possible to go back.
They got short shrift and soon gave up the idea. The mood of
uncertainty was not improved when the ship picked up survivors
from a torpedoed vessel, reminding the men of the lurking U-boats.
They had barely left Liverpool when inboard hazards soon surfaced.
The food, it was agreed by those with experience, was worse than
Russian prison fare. Then, the men seemed to be spending day and
night playing cards, and it soon emerged that some professional card
sharps had been netted for military service along with the innocents
who were being fleeced of their meagre savings. Fights broke out.

The political émigrés who had experience of the 1905 Revolution, trade union organisers and a number of intellectuals discussed what might happen when they reached Archangel, and they agreed that if they were not organised they would be led by the nose. Accordingly, a committee of some forty individuals was formed, with a smaller one to deal with the problems that were arising on board. The card sharps, when offered the choice of handing back their victims' money or swimming back to Liverpool, quickly took the dry option and a degree of peace was restored. Nothing could be done about the food, even after breaking into the ship's bakery in search of something edible.

As they steamed further north, the seas mounted, the wind turned icy and thoughts of the future grew bleaker, though the crew assured them that no submarine could attack in such conditions. When the ships left the Arctic Ocean and entered the straits of Murman, the men saw snow at sea level. The White Sea itself begins to freeze by late September. After about two weeks on board, the men were eager to stand on dry, stable land, maybe find a hot bath and a decent meal. As the ships, escorted by Russian naval vessels, manoeuvred through the mined fjord of the Northern Dvina towards Archangel, bottles of whisky appeared and the men celebrated their safe arrival and waited to be taken ashore.

But there was a hold-up. One day passed, then another and another. For five days they waited in a state of limbo, just a few hundred yards from the dockside. The emergence of a British naval officer caused momentary panic, but nothing came of it. Representations to the captain (who was friendly to his passengers and may have been the source of the celebratory Scotch) produced no results. According to three unprompted survivors, interviewed in different places and on different days, eventually two revolutionaries, armed with revolvers, forced the captain to lower a lifeboat and accompany a four-man deputation to see the mayor of the city to find out why the passengers were not being allowed to disembark. They returned to the ship with a promise that within two days they would be supplied with food and put on board trains to Moscow.

What the Conventionists did not know, and what no one in authority saw fit to tell them, was that by the late summer of 1917 the city of Archangel was already bursting at the seams, with returnees arriving by ship and emigrants arriving by rail. Accustomed to exercising draconian rules in order to control transitting migrants, the local authorities tried using familiar methods to manage this latest influx. Trainborne arrivals were off-loaded at Isakagorka to await embarkation at Bakaritsa, a few miles from Archangel in the estuary, where they were housed in workers' huts, lying empty since the early summer, and where there were communal bath-houses. Shipborne arrivals, including the Conventionists, were kept onboard until they could be loaded straight onto the trains that would take them and their problems somewhere else.

The need to control the movement of these comparatively large numbers – hundreds *and* thousands, rather than the hundreds *of* thousands who would soon inundate the southern Russian ports – became all the more urgent when orders came from the ministry of the interior on 23 September not to allow these returnees to travel to Moscow and Petrograd, in view of the crisis of accommodation and food supply in both those large centres. The Provisional government allocated funds to assist Archangel as a holding centre, and although many Conventionists were off-loaded at Bakaritsa and put on trains at Isakagorka before they could become a burden on the city, many were nevertheless sent on to Moscow, despite the government's declared intentions. Such was the organisational disarray.

Considering the whole purpose of the Convention, it was an extraordinary act of bureaucratic negligence that the British authorities had given the men no papers of any kind to indicate who they were, or why they had turned up in Russia at all. Even their British aliens registration books had been taken from them by the police as they had boarded the ship in Liverpool, although the more astute among them had managed to hang onto this document for future use. Some men had their original Russian passports. My father had his Russian Army discharge book, issued in 1906 after four years of military service, and he wisely kept this safely with him from the time he left London to the time he would return two and a half years later. Many others did the same.

Eventually, the Archangel port authority processed the Conventionists for entry into Russia, examined whatever bits of papers the men could produce and stamped them, for example, 'Arrived 11 [24 New Style] September 1917'. On the same day, the consul reported that information concerning the arrivals had been passed to the local Russian military governor, indicating that he at least knew who they were and why they had been sent, but giving no further details. The local press woke up to the fact that the trickle of returning Russians who had been passing through Archangel since the early summer had now reached significant numbers. On 17/30 September it reported that émigrés from America, France and other Allied states were arriving in Archangel: 'Among the passengers who arrived on the steamer *Kursk* there were about 50 fighters for freedom. About 3,000 have arrived and about 30,000 are expected. The majority are Jews who have refused military service in Allied countries.'

Having registered the men's arrival, the next question was what to do with them. They had been transported to Russia to be put into Russian Army uniform and sent to fight. But even by late September – to say nothing of late October when the last shipments arrived – the Russian Army barely existed, Russia's war was all but over. And such contact as there may have been with Russian military authorities would be tangential, at best. At the start of the shipments, at the end of August, Nabokov had cabled the Provisional government, warning of the imminent arrival at Archangel of the steamship *Bienvenue*, carrying ninety-four Russians liable for military service: 'I consider it my duty to point out', Nabokov had written, 'that these people represent a very unreliable element and should be kept under close supervision.' At the same time, Russian military intelligence in Petrograd had been receiving reports that Russian émigrés of various types were arriving at Archangel and coming on by train to Petrograd. Neither notice of their imminent arrival nor instructions on what to do with them had been issued. They were coming without papers or an escort. Elsewhere in the capital, at a railway goods yard, a contingent of nearly 600 émigrés with wives and children had arrived, this time with military escort. Here, the military intelligence officer knew it was his duty to check the arrivals, and 'anyone who is not suspected of being a spy will be given back their passports with a note to report to the local army chief for military service'.

The Provisional government wanted to carry out its responsibilities towards its Allies in good conscience. Among its first acts it had assumed the cost of repatriating political exiles and émigrés, and had allocated two million roubles to the foreign ministry for this task. But the handling of recruitment was in the hands of the war ministry, where, despite domestic chaos and the disintegration of the army, new policies on the mobilisation of irregular categories continued to be made, incredibly, as late as mid-October. Political émigrés, for instance, if they could prove their bona fides, were allowed forty days after arriving in Russia in which to arrange their affairs before joining up, and blank forms were issued to the port authorities on which men could make application and be given a date for their enlistment. As if on the eve of the October/November Revolution political émigrés would agree to obey powerless officials!

It is surprising that the Russian military were still maintaining regulations on military service at all. For instance, in mid-September the army commander in Irkutsk, a major centre of the Russian exile administration in eastern Siberia, informed the war ministry that hard labour convicts were protesting against being conscripted before their civil and political rights had been restored to them: 'They are threatening disorder. Send instructions.' And in the same month, when the Russian consul in Copenhagen asked for guidance on local Russians of military age, he was told not to try too hard to ascertain whether a man was or was not a true political exile: 'It's too difficult to prove, or to establish the real reasons.' The law was to be applied: they should simply be sent home for army service.

The Provisional government had introduced the forty-day rule to give returning political émigrés time to settle their affairs and look after their families before enlisting. The Petrograd commandant seems to have been unaware of this rule, and many returnees on their way from Archangel to Moscow were detained in Petrograd where they were denied deferment and enlisted straightaway. Other local authorities seem to have been equally oblivious of this rule. The Petrograd Soviet, watchful of any over-zealous war effort on the government's part, duly complained, and received a reassuring reply from the war ministry that returning émigrés who could provide proof that they were political émigrés would be given the forty days deferment from the date of their arrival in Russia, for example, for those entering from Sweden from their arrival at Torneo, for those coming by sea from their arrival at Archangel. The entry stamp in their passports would serve for this. As for non-political émigrés now arriving in Russia, having applied to serve in the Russian Army for the duration of the war, they were subject to immediate call-up.

* * *

One Sergeant Roger S. Clark of the 310th US Army Engineers, finding himself in Archangel at Christmas 1918 as part of the Intervention forces, immortalised his feelings about Russia in general and Archangel in particular in a poem which, inspired perhaps by the anonymous epic of *Eskimo Nell,* succeeds in conveying something of the forlorn character of the place. Having completed the Creation, God 'made on the shores of the Arctic/ a great international dump' he called Russia … 'And then, feeling glum and sarcastic,/ because it was Saturday night,/ He spotted the nastiest corner/ and called it "Archangel", for spite!/ … It's the home of the glop and the bohunk/ and herring and mud-colored crows/ … the average American soldier/ would rather be quartered in Hell!'

It is unlikely that any of the returnees, of whatever category, felt that landing in Archangel was like coming 'home'. Situated on the Northern Dvina at the site of a monastery founded in 1583, traditionally Archangel was not the port of choice for Russians leaving the country, nor the entry port of choice for Westerners, other than for merchants landing their wares. But the Baltic, which was the preferred sea route into Russia, was blockaded by the Germans, and only the northern route was now accessible. As the anglicised form of Arkhangel'sk suggests, the town had long been known as a port for the trade of the Muscovy Company, founded by the merchant explorer Richard Chancellor in the middle of the sixteenth century. It was partly eclipsed when St Petersburg was founded at the beginning of the eighteenth century, but in the period before the First World War at least 500 ships called annually. Construction of the naval base and port of Murmansk, where the Gulf Stream keeps the Arctic coast above Archangel ice-free, was begun only in 1915, which meant that Archangel would retain its importance for some time to come.

Even before the Revolution, the population of the entire vast province had not exceeded 345,000, while the city's inhabitants numbered about 48,000. Russians accounted for well over 90 per cent of the local population, with some small Finnic tribes making up the rest. There were 251 Jews in the province, and 248 of them lived in the city, alongside the many foreigners, mostly British and German, who did business there. Since Archangel was not in the Pale of Jewish Settlement, these Jews were mostly the servants of the very few prosperous Jewish merchants who were allowed to reside anywhere in Russia. There was little industry, except timber and fishing, and all the export trade was in the hands of foreign residents and Jews. The abolition of the Pale by the Provisional government in 1917 did not prompt a flood of Jewish migration to Archangel, as it did to Petrograd and Moscow, but the returning émigrés and the Conventionists had a certain impact on the Jewish life of the port city.

In late September the local press gave advance notice that on 22

October a Jewish school and high school would be opened in the Jewish community house. Permission to establish a school had been sought in 1880, but the government had rejected the application on the grounds that Archangel was not in the Pale. It had not been tsarist policy to encourage Jewish development in Russia proper, and the Jewish children of Archangel must have gone to Russian schools. In the Russia of 1917, described by Lenin as 'the freest country in the world', the community could act without hindrance. As further evidence that the sudden flurry of activity in the port city was having its effect on the local economy, the press reported that 'foreigners arriving in Archangel are buying property, e.g. an English company has bought a large house from Citizen Meyer on Troitsky Prospekt. The price is rumoured to be 300,000 roubles'. Some of the returning Russians may have been acting on behalf of British companies.

Meanwhile, the Conventionists were each given some salted herring, a half-pound bag of sugar, some tea and a can for the boiling water to be found at all stations, if not on the train itself, and a five-pound loaf of black bread, the staple of every Russian meal.* They were then loaded into *teplushki* (heated wagons), which were converted cattle trucks with a small stove in the centre and two sleeping platforms, in effect double bunks, slung at each end. No further processing by officials took place at this stage.

Unlike the political returnees of a month or so earlier, the Conventionists who arrived in late September were routed straight to Moscow, avoiding Petrograd but halting briefly at Vologda, a junction on the Moscow–Archangel railway, a dead little centre with an ancient fortress on the high bank of a river of the same name. Like Archangel, the town had been eclipsed as a trading centre by the rise of St Petersburg and nothing much had happened there since the time of Ivan the Terrible. Those who came on the last shipments, arriving in October, were deposited at Vologda, either as a response to demands from the authorities seeking to enforce the military aim of the exercise, or, more likely, to relieve pressure elsewhere.

* * *

---

* In the Russian Army, soldiers were issued with a daily ration of three pounds of bread, but a complex system of 'distribution' ensured that they received only a portion, with the accumulated 'credit' paid out in cash twice yearly and amounting to about seventeen kopecks, but only after each level of command, from deputy company commander down to platoon sergeants, had taken their cut. Soldiers also used their bread ration as currency, like cigarettes in prison.

How the Conventionists fared inside Russia is no longer a collective story, or not entirely, at least. The October/November Revolution of 1917 and the Civil War that followed it, while they may be described and analysed in terms of their effect on groups, classes and whole nations, created a setting in which luck and personal judgment, as much as the initiative and efficiency of officials, often played a crucial part in the fate of a man. This certainly applies to the groups of Conventionists who arrived in Russia between August and October, when even their processing on entering Russia at Archangel was not regulated by any consistent authority, and clearly had not been locally planned in advance. The transport officials handling the men had been mostly left in the dark by the Provisional government, which had more pressing demands on its attention at the time.

Some of the groups arriving earlier in the summer disembarked at Murmansk – which remains a blank page in this narrative – and entrained for Petrograd. Those which landed at Archangel took the direct line for Moscow, stopping at Vologda for an hour where they were given fresh supplies of tea and bread before going on. The pressure on facilities was steadily reduced at Archangel by sending the Conventionists on to the capitals, but the central authorities were soon keen to offload these new burdens and decided to divert the groups to points east, particularly to Chelyabinsk in western Siberia, the junction linking the European railway system to the Trans-Siberian.

Those who came later on the *Tsaritsa*'s second voyage in late October had a tale to tell. About 1,000 of them had been waiting in a camp in Lancashire, their earlier departure having been postponed through damage to the ship. Disembarking in the evening, they found Archangel cold, dark and milling with soldiers and sailors, many of them refugees or deserters from the recently defeated Riga Front. Old lags among this ragtag mob offered to buy the superior English overcoats, boots and watches from the new arrivals, and many of the innocents took the opportunity to fill their wallets with what they assumed to be useful local currency. What they did not know was that the value of Russian paper roubles had fallen to near-worthless as the war had practically destroyed the domestic economy and prices had become inflated by hundreds of percentage points. The entire floor of Archangel station building was turned into a bazaar. The hall, though well heated, provided no food and at midnight the group boarded an outgoing train, thirty to a carriage, the usual *teplushki*. Two candles provided the sole source of lighting. The standard ration of black bread and salted herring was distributed at some stage, and the customary two buckets provided, one with water for the tea and the other for more basic needs.

Whenever the train stopped, which it did at every village station, there would be a mad rush by the men to find food. On one such occasion, since it was never known how long the train would wait, several were left behind, their fate forever lost in the God-forsaken north of Russia. It began to snow as the train reached Vologda. Here, in this relatively large town, some seized the chance to send a telegram home with reassuring news, while the socialist intellectuals went in search of newspapers, usually in vain. Ramshackle shops and a primitive café, run by local Jews, sold black bread and tea. In conversation with the Russian soldiers, the Conventionists learned that desertion was rife. The previous day, for instance, 20,000 men had entrained for the front, but at every stop several hundred had quietly left the train taking their rifles and belongings with them, and scattered to different towns for refuge from the authorities, such as they were, their own officers being practically helpless by now. Any officer who tried to remonstrate with them found himself flung from the moving train without ceremony.

Vologda had been chosen as a convenient mid-point between Archangel and Moscow where the returnees were to be given travel documents, rail tickets and permits to go where they wished. Those whose native towns were in the western and north-western provinces were prevented by the war from going there, while men from the south could choose any of the major cities there, such as Odessa and Ekaterinoslav. Those with no preferences were sent straight on from Vologda to Omsk, via Chelyabinsk, and from there to various other towns in Siberia. On 6 November, most of the 1,000 men from the *Tsaritsa* carried on to Chelyabinsk, where better food and a hot bath awaited them.*

Those who waited behind in Vologda did so in conditions described by a Commissar Mazey who had been dispatched by the regional committee of the All-Russian Union of Towns to sort things out. This voluntary body had survived the fall of the Tsar and was trying to continue its work of alleviating public distress wherever it

---

* Much of this account comes from the scrapbook of an unnamed Conventionist, some of which was published in *The Shanghai Weekly* on 9 March 1918.

was to be found. Nothing is known about Mazey, except that he bore the name of an eminent Moscow rabbi, Yakov Mazey who was active in Jewish affairs, specifically Russian settlements in Palestine before 1914. It is not inconceivable that this was the same Mazey. In any event, our Mazey was undoubtedly a Jew and his arrival at Vologda suggests that a regional agency, if not the government itself, had sent him to assess this novel situation in the belief that he might have special insight.

Mazey found that the men were made up of three groups, Jews, Lithuanians and Poles, the Jews being in the majority. The designation 'Poles' is unexpected. The only 'Poles' involved in the Convention were the Russian Jews who, having been born in Polish provinces under Russian control, perhaps speaking better Polish than Russian, might have defined themselves as Poles. But they had no Polish legal status, since none existed until a year or so later, when Poland at last achieved her long-denied independence. The Lithuanians discovered by Mazey were described as aged between twenty-five and forty, many of them had lived a long time in Britain, most of them having completely severed their ties with Russia and knowing no Russian. These were in fact the coal-miners of Lanark, Lithuanian immigrants with Russian nationality described by Murdoch Rodgers, without British friends in high places and unknown to public opinion. They had been deported en masse to Russia with unprecedented dispatch and with scarcely a public murmur, once the Convention was in place in the summer of 1917. About 1,200 men were shipped to Russia, but no more than a third of them were eventually able to return to the families that had survived their absence in the direst of conditions in Scotland.

Originally, in order not to overload the system it had been intended to dispatch the returnees from Archangel in groups of 300, and when Mazey arrived in Vologda he found a party of about 1,250 emigrants 'living like wild animals'. Using the heated goods wagons as their quarters, and finding the supply of food reasonable, the men were trying to survive the northern winter in the same summer clothes they had been wearing on embarkation in England. Many had not changed their linen in eight weeks. Apparently the effect on the 'intellectuals' among them had been appalling. Mazey's recommendation was that the men be kept at Vologda temporarily, then divided up into manageable groups and sent back to Britain. Like the regime he represented, Mazey was well intentioned but out of touch with reality. All this was described in letters received by or passed on to the Yiddish newspaper *Unzer Leben* (Our Life) in Shanghai, and published in *Tsait* (Time), another Yiddish organ, on 21 February 1918.

Mazey, whose plan to move the Conventionists as soon as possible was motivated by humanitarian considerations, soon realised that his foundlings had ideas of their own. About 200 of the original contingent had managed to get their meagre belongings through customs in Archangel and gone straight to Moscow. (It is surprising to learn that, even in late summer the customs service was functioning at all. What would they have been looking for, what excise duties were being levied and on whose authority?) The majority were still waiting for their baggage to come from Archangel and they had no intention of going on anywhere until it was restored to them. For some it represented all their worldly goods. They had not even wanted to leave Archangel without it, but they had been promised that it would follow them to Vologda at once. Now they resisted similar assurances, convinced that the customs officials in Archangel would not bother to send it on, especially if they abandoned Vologda for more remote destinations. They also pointed out that they had been given no receipts for their baggage and that much of it was unlabelled. When two new groups of returnees, numbering 818 and 900 men, turned up and declared that they, too, would go no further without their baggage, the icy air turned blue with invective.

The plan to get the travellers back home was dropped in favour of one that envisaged sending them all in one large group to Omsk, whither their baggage would be shipped soon after. A group of twenty men would be left at Vologda to ensure that the plan was carried out. When the men would not agree to this, it was decided to move them out against their will, although the reports do not indicate what means were used to effect this. In any event, at eight o'clock one morning the train began to move, and when the passengers, still asleep in the wagons, realised what was happening they started jumping out. In the end, 700 went on to Omsk, leaving about 500 behind in Vologda. It seems likely that the Omsk-bound group were the Lithuanian miners from Lanarkshire. A letter from one such unfortunate was published in the *North-East Lanark Gazette* on 18 January 1918, and forwarded by the Lanarkshire chief constable to the Home Office. They in turn showed it to

Vladimir Jabotinsky as a propaganda weapon to be used in the Yiddish press to discourage further would-be returnees and encourage recruits for the Jewish Legion then being formed in Britain for service in Palestine.

The Lithuanian miner in Omsk had written that he had no idea when he would get out. They could find no work, and some of the 'head ones' were saying they might still have to join the army. The Lithuanians were at a loss to know what might happen next. Some of them, mainly the married ones, had located a British consulate and were hoping for its assistance in getting them back to Scotland. Only a couple of miles from the railway station where they were kicking their heels, Omsk was the administrative centre of the Siberian military district, and the fear of enlistment was plainly real. The Lithuanians took the view that if they were threatened with conscription they would refuse and would try to get back and join the British Army. The fact that only a quarter of them, about 300 men, got back to Scotland raises the possibility that a good many of them may well have been recruited locally. The letter went on:

> We were all fooled by our agitators about the first trip that went away from London; they told us that we wouldn't need to join the army, that there was plenty of work and good money; but we have found out everything to be different. If we had only known that the country was in such a state we would never have left Scotland. If everything was all settled up it might be alright to live here, but at the present moment it's not worth it; it is so awfully cold here just now, 20 degrees of frost. Such weather! I would have Scotland before this at any price!

The choice on offer had not been between Scotland and Russia, but the British or Russian armies. The Lithuanians, although they were an extraordinarily tight-knit community, had – like the Jews – been subjected to contrary propaganda and agitation by their priests and their socialist leaders. The priests had encouraged them to join the British Army to show loyalty to their adopted country, while the socialists, in league with the British Left, had exhorted them to follow exactly the same practices as the Jews, that is, first refuse, then insist on returning to Russia. By comparison with the Jews, the Lithuanians were an isolated group, far fewer in number, and their very cohesion made it all the easier for the police to carry out the deportation in near-secrecy and totality. Now, the hardships of life in Siberia might well have seemed a greater evil than the once-dreaded Western Front. It is surprising that this letter got through with even the minimal information about its place of origin, as MI5 censors reported that letters from Conventionists in Russia were arriving with military and naval addresses deleted, it was assumed, by a Russian civil authority.

Back in Vologda, meanwhile, the baggage finally arrived from Archangel, together with the news that customs had not found the time to examine it after all and that it must be sent straight on to Chelyabinsk by the Trans-Siberian express. Whatever the condition of the clothes that had been left crushed in cheap cardboard suitcases or tied in bundles in a damp, freezing customs shed at Archangel, the men wanted them and needed them, but were not allowed to have them. Despite Mazey's best efforts to have the bags restored to their owners without customs' clearance, most of the group eventually gave up and joined the train that was carrying their belongings to Chelyabinsk. Some had found work and even wives in Vologda and stayed behind, perhaps forever, and others went elsewhere in the wake of their possessions.

For most Conventionists, then, the war seemed to have been successfully avoided. Now, they were being left to fend for themselves in revolutionary Russia, with only a railway warrant and the scraps of documents they had managed to hang on to. With the western provinces out of bounds, some of the more adventurous decided to try a round-the-world route, eastwards. They must have had the foresight to bring with them sufficiently warm clothing to survive a Siberian winter, as they set out towards China. Luckily, Jews had settled in many of the towns and cities which had sprung up along the Trans-Siberian Railway and they provided the customary help and hospitality to any Jew wandering far from home. Some of the new arrivals might well have become settlers themselves, and some must have fallen by the wayside, as arriving in China felt like coming to the Promised Land to any Conventionist who made it.

At least one of the 'Trans-Siberians' acquired a brand new Russian passport in December 1918, made his way back to the western side of the Urals, turned south to Odessa and joined the French Foreign Legion, returning to his family in London after five years of defending the French Empire in North Africa. Many, especially those with families and connections in Ukraine and the

Crimea, like my father and his brother, also headed south. Wherever they eventually chose to go, the Conventionists were now emphatically 'back home', and their separate fates would rest only partly in their own hands. The next and last part of the story is mostly what the survivors related, and is set against a background of chaos, violence of both an arbitrary and organised kind, hunger and disease, bad luck and extraordinary good fortune.

7 Surviving Revolution

Reconstructing precisely what happened to any of the Conventionists during the years they spent in Russia is limited by the paucity of personal documents, but also because their arrival in Russia coincided with the greatest upheaval in that country's history, when record-keeping was not the highest priority; and finally, because only a few of them survived long enough to be found and interviewed. What they related of their experience, and what their families were able to add, is of course primary material, but like all 'archives' they acquire added veracity when they are corroborated, whether by other survivors or by documents. Letters, scattered newspaper reports and military certificates add to the general picture of the kinds of experience the Conventionists typically had in the course of the odysseys forced on them by the Convention. While the number of men who went back is fairly certain, the number of those who got out of Russia and back to their adopted homeland of Britain is unknown, as is the number and fate of those who died in Russia, or of those who embraced the Soviet Union and settled for better or worse.

The Conventionists arrived in Russia when the disintegration of the old tsarist order was virtually complete. The October/November Revolution followed soon after their arrival. Thereafter, for almost three years the chaos of the Civil War completed the destructive effects of the First World War that had already ravaged the economy. A hapless group of refugees forced back to the land they had recently fled, they found themselves at the mercy of events barely less momentous than the turmoil on the Western Front, thrown from one crisis to another and trying to survive as the fabric of the Russian state unravelled. The war effectively ended for the Russians in December 1917 when they agreed an armistice with the Germans, and then signed the Treaty of Brest-Litovsk in March 1918. But it would be two or three years before any Conventionist was able to get out of the country and back to Britain, and some did not make it until the late 1920s.

Travelling inside Russia during revolution and civil war required physical strength, willpower, native wit and a lot of luck. A journey of a couple of hundred miles might take two weeks or more, so numerous were the hazards, and so overloaded the railways, packed with soldiers and refugees moving in all directions. And it was not only the railways that were close to breakdown: by late 1917 virtually the entire system of state administration was going the same way, especially that of the Russian Army. In these conditions, the story of the Conventionists becomes as fragmented as its setting. While many of them tried to stick together, believing in safety in numbers, the forces of circumstance sent them in various directions and to varied fates. At different times, the authorities dispatched different groups to different concentration points, partly because the army they had ostensibly come to join was falling apart, partly because no one knew what else to do with them, and possibly because a group of 3,000 potential new recruits would have constituted a logistical problem for officials who were still nominally in charge of a military organisation that was hanging by a thread, if at all. Scattered to different places after their arrival in Archangel, the Conventionists gravitated towards towns that were either familiar to them, or that seemed to offer the best chance of getting back to Britain. Archangel itself remained a magnet for many, while others aimed for Moscow, Siberia and the Far East. But the majority headed south to the Ukrainian provinces, to Odessa and the Crimea.

The returnees who had been routed directly to Moscow in September were comparatively lucky, perhaps because it would not become the capital of Russia until March 1918, and was not yet the centre of army administration. The city authorities were anxious to send the Conventionists on their way somewhere, anywhere, else. Riding the train from Archangel, it was some time before they saw any obvious signs of the Revolution, or the chaos that came to characterise it. The railway stations along the route looked much like Russian railway stations anywhere, and were familiar to those who had travelled the railways only a few years earlier, either as departing emigrants or conscripts on their way to an army posting or, like my father, to war in Manchuria.

Some vestiges of the administration set up by the Provisional government still functioned, for instance at Vologda, but as they neared Moscow the travellers noticed red flags and revolutionary slogans, and packs of soldiers crowding the platforms. The only evidence of the treatment they received on reaching Moscow is provided by distant recollection. Only one survivor claimed they were met by some sort of military authority, and even that they were medically examined. Most recalled no military authority whatever, and no medical, but thought it possible the city soviet had stepped in to handle the large number of unexpected new arrivals. They were housed in a large dormitory, a school, perhaps, or an old people's home, certainly somewhere near the city centre, but no one could remember much more about it than its very large kitchen.

Feeling completely disoriented, with no idea of what was to happen to them, the men wandered about the city in small groups, trying not to make themselves conspicuous, and waiting for the 'next episode'. My father remembered the sights of Moscow, especially the Kremlin and the crowds he joined to listen to revolutionary speeches on street corners. Had he been routed to Petrograd he certainly would have witnessed stellar performances of revolutionary oratory, but Moscow, though still somewhat provincial by comparison, had many Bolshevik firebrands who would emerge as senior figures. What money he had in his pocket he did not waste on tram fares: like any other working man of his age and means, he was accustomed to walking for miles. The ship's committee of the *Kursk* still functioned and it was decided that, despite the risk of drawing the wrong kind of attention to themselves, a deputation should go to the defence commissariat for 'clarification'. The residual military administration was preoccupied with the house-keeping problems of the self-demobilising soldiery: accommodation, food coupons, rail tickets. No mention was made about recruiting the Conventionists, and their representatives were told to bring their comrades and line up for the same handouts.

Even though the recruiting authorities were still receiving enquiries from foreign embassies, asking whether such and such locally resident Russian citizen should be apprehended and sent back for military service, for the Conventionists kicking their heels in Moscow one thing was crystal clear: now that the Bolsheviks had seized power the Convention was meaningless and no one had the least intention of applying it in Russia.* The Conventionists were told they should choose a destination and railway warrants would be issued at once.

---

* On 25 February 1918, the mobilisation department of the 'war ministry' – still so named and still using Provisional government headed paper, though on whose authority and under what 'minister' is unclear – noted, in connection with the military service of Russians in Alexandria, Egypt, that 'as demobilisation seems to have become a fact of life, they ought to let recalcitrant cases drop'.

While the majority went south, others went back to the familiarity of Archangel, and some went east. With the west still a war zone, the Trans-Siberian Railway seemed to offer an escape route to the east, a long, long road to the exit from Russia at Vladivostok on the Pacific Ocean, and many desperate thousands of refugees crowded station platforms all the way along the line, hoping for a safe passage. But the railway itself became a battle zone of the Civil War that erupted in 1918, as a profusion of armed units of the most varied political stripe and strength fought for control of this vital line of communication at both ends of it. Refugees fleeing the conflicts that arose at the eastern end of the line met refugees coming the other way, adding to the congestion along the length of the great railway. The Bolsheviks' armoured trains – Trotsky's came to symbolise the march of the Revolution – were an early sign that they understood the vital importance of Russia's railways, and they soon installed their own police, the Cheka, on mainline trains. Breakdowns and stoppages were frequent, and any Conventionist hoping to reach his goal by the Trans-Siberian route was in for as turbulent a time as those who opted for the south.

Standing at the eastern end of the railway, Vladivostok became both a temporary haven and an escape hatch. By 1919 Vladivostok's population had leapt from 97,000 to 410,000, as hordes of refugees flocked there in the wake of the retreating White Army. Among them were close to 1,000 members of the cultural institutions of Petrograd and Moscow – musicians, actors, several symphony orchestras and the staffs of a number of art magazines. After the Bolsheviks gained control of the region, most of these got out and made their way to China, Australia, the USA and Western Europe, and along with them went most of the city's other temporary asylum-seekers. By 1926 the population had fallen back to 108,000.

The experience of one of the east-bound Conventionists is probably typical of many others. Samuel Goldman left Glasgow in September 1917 and, after journeying from Archangel to Vologda, took the train to Chelyabinsk, where he remained for several months, getting his bearings, working at whatever manual labour came his way to pay for shelter, a crust and some vital winter clothing, and waiting for an opportunity to continue his journey eastwards. Two years later, in October 1919, the US consul in the port of Kobe, Japan, issued a certificate of discharge to a seaman who had just left his ship, the *Heffron*, recently arrived from

Vladivostok. This seaman went by the name of Samuel Mann. He was 38 years old, of Russian nationality, and was described as being 'of good character and ability'. He had left his ship 'by mutual consent' of the captain. According to an unstamped document, issued by a Sergeant G. E. Townsend, until June 1919 Samuel Mann had been working for several months as a carpenter under the charge of the 'British Mission on Russian Island, Siberia'.

Russian Island, about seven by eight miles in size and standing at the entrance to Peter the Great Bay to the south of Vladivostok, was the main bastion protecting the sea approaches to Russia's Pacific coast from the direction of Japan. Densely covered in forest and deep valleys, the island was dominated by Russian Hill which at a height of 1,000 feet provided a commanding view over a wide expanse of the Sea of Japan. Beginning in the late nineteenth century, and especially after the loss of Port Arthur at the beginning of the Russo-Japanese War, the Russians had steadily reinforced and ramified their defences on Russian Island with hill forts and shore batteries – more than 100 fortifications and a huge garrison of 90,000 men. On 31 December 1917, Japanese, American and British cruisers entered Golden Horn Bay off Vladivostok and in April 1918, on the pretext of protecting their citizens, they landed their troops on Russian Island, among them the good Sergeant Townsend whose staff was soon supplemented by the carpentry skills of Samuel Mann. Russian Island was at the time the headquarters and chief Far Eastern base of the White forces under Admiral Kolchak.

According to documents shown to me by his family, the Samuel Goldman who left Glasgow in 1917 was the self-same Samuel Mann. He had spent more than a year getting through Siberia, in conditions and circumstances that remain unknown, found work at the British garrison on Russian Island in late 1918 or early 1919, got a job on board the *Heffron* until October, crossed the Pacific to San Francisco, probably working as a ship's hand again, traversed the United States and eventually returned to his adopted homeland of Scotland in the early 1920s. Given the anti-Bolshevik, anti-Russian climate in Britain, his 'friendly alien' status was now less certain, and his re-entry into Britain was made possible only by the handwritten, unstamped testimonial of the sergeant-carpenter for whom he had worked on Russian Island.

Those who went south seemed right to assume they had the best chance of surviving, or even getting back home, but the going was far from smooth, and 'exemption' from military service was also not guaranteed. For instance, Abraham Aspess, a shoe uppers-maker, was one of those who chose the Russia of 1917 as a safe bet, but a year later he found himself in the Red Army. Born in Lublin, south-eastern Poland, and therefore cut off from his family home, with a large group of Conventionists he made his way to an uncle in Ekaterinoslav (Dnipropetrovsk today) in Ukraine where he got work in a shoe factory. The group – the number varied between 30 and 70 – had stuck together, and when the Civil War broke out they had joined the 1st International Regiment, a multi-national blend of about 8,000 men, including Jews, Poles, and Czech and German ex-prisoners of war.

When I interviewed Chone Simon in his retirement home in Southend-on-Sea, he told me, with unexplained tears in his eyes, that going back to Russia in 1917 had been 'the worst thing I ever did in my life': the episode had obviously preyed on his mind for decades, and he was not too sure he wanted to dredge it all up and lay it out for a stranger, though a stranger is often the best audience for painful memories, and his account turned out to be one of the most detailed I heard from the survivors. One of the Ekaterinoslav group, his degree of recall was remarkable, his story not only hung together but both corroborated and was itself corroborated by the accounts of other survivors.

He had returned to Russia in August with the first small group of 52 in the *Pollern*, thinking that at last he was going to witness the realisation of a dream, a free Russia where everyone was equal. Instead he found himself in a waking nightmare. The casual violence and brutal behaviour he saw meted out by Russian troops on the trains, some of it aimed at his companions, reinforced his determination to avoid the Russian Army. In search of a safe billet, he went to a sister in Orsha, in the north-east of what would become Belorussia (Belarus) and to the east of German-occupied territory. Afraid that he might still be picked up by the authorities for military service, he moved on to another sister in Lozna, in the same Vitebsk Province. False passports were evidently not too hard to come by: Count Lobanov-Rostovsky recalled being offered a choice of five by a friend. With substantially less local influence than the Count, Simon managed to acquire just one, and with it a degree of protection against enlistment and other unpleasantness. Ownership of a false passport, whether you were the scion of an ancient noble family or an indigent Jewish refugee, created a smokescreen of sufficient duration to allow you (in the absence of telephones) to get away from the authorities while your details were being checked. It also enabled Simon to move on to Ekaterinoslav where he remained until General Anton Denikin's White army captured the region in the summer of 1919.

In the late nineteenth century, when industrialisation took off in Russia, Ekaterinoslav had expanded from a small market town into a major city. Centred on the production of coal and steel, it had spawned countless service and small industries which attracted workers from all parts of Russia, taking the population from about 20,000 in the 1860s to 200,000 in 1914. In the 1890s the north-western provinces of the Pale were suffering from over-supply of the traditional Jewish trades and professions, especially in the clothing industry, and despite the legal obstacles to changing one's place of residence, Jews had migrated steadily to the new opportunities opening up in the south: in 1914 Jews numbered close to 70,000 or 34 per cent of Ekaterinoslav's population, the highest proportion of any city in the region, exceeding even Odessa's by 2 per cent.

Situated in the central part of Ukraine, in the years 1918 to 1920 Ekaterinoslav turned out to be one of the worst choices the Conventionists could have made in their search for a temporary haven. Between various Ukrainian nationalist armed factions, as well as the Germans, the White armies and the Bolsheviks, the city changed hands no less than twenty-five times, and occasionally several rival governments wrestled to administer it simultaneously. In the summer of 1919, when Denikin's forces were preparing their assault, the Bolsheviks rounded up all the able-bodied men they could find. Chone Simon and his friends were marched off from the marketplace to a barracks where Trotsky happened to be giving one of his rallying speeches. It was too crowded for Simon and the others to get in to see the great man, but they were issued with rifles and told to report next morning to be sent to the front. The band of Conventionist brothers were not quite ready to surrender the right not to bear arms – a right for which they had defied the British government and braved the perils of the North Sea – and so next morning Simon and his life-long friend David Meyers hid in tall grass and waited for the troops to move off. He would later claim to have spent twelve hours in the Red Army as a non-combatant.

One of the most painful accounts was given by Leon Cohen, who had arrived in London just before the war as a single young man on his own, and had opted to return to Russia, arriving in Archangel in October 1917. After a spell in Moscow, he had wandered aimlessly from one temporary shelter to another, mostly on his own, and by the time the Civil War began he had managed to get to his father's home in a village near Odessa, where he found his family starving and one of his young sisters seriously ill. She died soon after his arrival. In the absence of bread, the family had been eating grass and it was not long before both his parents crawled into their bed and also died. Feeling desperate in the face of such misfortune and deprivation, Leon pulled himself together and left the village with his remaining sister. They found the British consul in Odessa, where he discovered that an aunt in London had been trying to locate him. Regrettably, he could not recall much detail of his time in Odessa, or even in Russia, beyond the trauma of the family deaths, but he seems to have spent a further year waiting for the British consul to do something. The fact that he had not served in any Allied army did not help. Eventually, the unhappy pair found themselves in a resettlement camp of sorts in Germany, where large numbers of other Jews were in the same boat, and from there they eventually got back to London. Dredging up the memory of these events had a visibly depressing effect on him. Reluctant to press him for further details, I terminated our conversation.

If most of Poland and the western provinces were out of bounds in the summer of 1917, the south of Russia and the Crimea were not long to remain havens of rest and security, whether for the civilian or military population, or any other categories in between, such as the Conventionists. Nor were they the only 'visitors' faced with the turmoil and feeling an urgent need to leave the country by whatever means they could find. By the summer of 1918 various anti-Bolshevik volunteer armies had been formed, soon to be known generically as 'White'. To add to the general confusion, Allied intervention forces had been sent to Russia to suppress the Bolsheviks and facilitate the establishment of a regime that would be friendly to the Allies and continue fighting the Germans. Some, like the French, had been in the south of Russia since before the Bolshevik Revolution, or had been brought there from the Turkish front to fight in the Russian Civil War, and they in particular were becoming increasingly politicised. The French soldiers who had mutinied in 1917 had been defending *la Patrie* itself, and they had no desire to be sent to the Turkish front. A year later, totally fed up with the war, in October 1918 a detachment of French soldiers in the Crimea rebelled and were ready to 'go Bolshevik'. By March 1919, the French in Odessa were in dire straits. They lacked food and there were fears for their security.

At the same time, a large contingent of French soldiers were brought to Odessa under guard and in a state of rebellion. They claimed to have been duped by their commandant who had told them, while en route from the front at Salonika, that the war was not over and that they must now fight the Germans who 'are playing at being the masters of Russia'. The commandant had distributed pamphlets giving an allegedly false picture of events in Russia, including horror stories about Bolshevik atrocities. And when they were sent off to fight they were told they would only be fighting bandits, not a revolutionary army. Now, they claimed, their eyes had been opened. Many had refused to go to the front, while those who went did so only through fear of punishment. French soldiers who had joined the White Volunteer Army were also refusing to fight the Bolsheviks, having been completely unaware of the existence of a disciplined Red Army. They now knew that the Soviets had an organised force 'with the support of the people', and they became sympathetic to the Revolution. But their chief desire remained to get home to France as soon as possible.

For their part, the Bolsheviks, who regularly beat up Poles and Greeks on the street, affected total respect for the French, 'their brothers in revolution'. Fleeing a Bolshevik gang, a Polish officer took refuge in a barracks occupied by French artillerymen. The French squadron commander had him thrown out onto the street where he was promptly murdered. Another French commander, to the mortification of his adjutant, gave all the squadron's food to the Bolsheviks as the French were leaving Odessa. In their haste to get out, the French also abandoned vast quantities of war supplies, most of which ended up in Bolshevik hands. Desertion and disobedience were rife. The crews of some of the French ships were on the brink of mutiny. At the end of March 1919 the military government in Constantinople decided that all Allied forces should be evacuated from Odessa, that 20,000 Russian refugees should be transported with them to Constantinople, and a force kept at Sebastopol for the time being.

By this time the Crimea had become a desperate last resort for countless Russians, military and civilian, attempting to escape the conditions and daily threat to life in the war-torn south. Hundreds of thousands of refugees had flooded into the Black Sea ports at Nikolaev, Novorossiisk and Sebastopol, while Batumi, which was Russia's chief oil-exporting port in the south-eastern corner of the Black Sea, became the main exit point from the Caucasus for refugees seeking salvation in Constantinople. Possession of a foreign visa or a passport became an almost impossible dream. Local newspapers carried advertisements offering everything from life-savings to a winter's supply of wood for such a document.

The Pale of Jewish Settlement had included the southern provinces of the old empire, but had excluded the naval base at Sebastopol and the resort towns of Yalta and Bakhchiserai, where the royal family and other aristocrats had had their summer palaces. Odessa, which was Russia's second port city after St Petersburg, was unique for the rich ethnic mixture of its half-million inhabitants. Russians and Ukrainians represented just over half the population, while Jews accounted for 32 per cent, or 160,000 – equal to the entire population of many other cities – and the remainder was made up of Greeks, Poles, Germans and Italians, and a variety of Caucasians. During the early part of the Civil War, the area under White control, with its enormous refugee problem and an army of disoriented soldiers, had become highly politicised, with an intensely anti-Semitic overtone. Not only were many of the leading Bolsheviks of Jewish origin – the most striking being Trotsky, the ubiquitous personification of the Red Army itself – but Jews were also becoming prominent in the new local administration. French refugees arriving in Constantinople in 1919 reported that 'Odessa's civilian police were mostly Jews, while the population was anti-Bolshevik'.

In fact, the Jews were under pressure from all the contending forces at work in the region. Abraham Aspess was one of a group of twenty Conventionists who were on the point of being shot by Whites as 'Jew Bolsheviks' when they were saved by French officers who arrived in the nick of time. Baron Peter Wrangel, who commanded the White forces in the Crimea and later in Constantinople, and who was widely regarded as one of the more civilised White generals, was a rabid anti-Semite. General Denikin, who controlled the White forces in the south, wanted to rally the populace against the 'Jewish commissars'. Ukrainian nationalists under Semion Petliura had the same aim but were even more vicious in their behaviour, and were indeed responsible for most of the anti-

Jewish atrocities which spread through the region. Polish army units and various bandit groups also targeted Jews.

Even parts of the Red Army harboured such attitudes. In Isaac Babel's stories based on the exploits of the 1st (Red) Cavalry Army, its non-fictional commander, Semyon Budyonny, was a simple Russian peasant who had loyally served the tsar as a soldier, and would now loyally serve the Soviet state as a soldier. With his peasant outlook intact, he boosted his forces by mobilising gangs of thugs who were allowed to carry out pogroms for their own profit and under his general command. Officially throughout the Soviet era, but in practice for the first twenty years, anti-Semitism was viewed as a reactionary mentality that had no place in the internationalist climate of the new Russia. The Civil War was officially being fought on class, not ethnic principles. But when Budyonny rode off to fight the Poles, Chone Simon, hiding in the long grass, heard him say, 'When we get back, we'll see what's to be done about the Jews.'

For about a year after the February/March Revolution, Jewish and non-Jewish political parties in Ukraine cooperated with unaccustomed camaraderie. Mostly of ethnic Russian or Jewish origin, local political leaders were working towards union with Russia within one big socialist federation. The October/November Revolution and especially the Russo-German armistice of December 1917 gave a powerful impulse to nationalist feeling and, encouraged by the occupying Germans, the Ukrainians changed direction and declared independence from Russia. In February 1918 the Germans signed a treaty with the Ukrainian National Republic and on the same day the Bolsheviks entered Kiev, the Ukrainian capital. Thereafter, until the end of 1920, Ukraine was the setting for the bloodiest scenes, with one regime succeeding another, culminating in a Ukrainian–Polish military alliance against Soviet Russia which brought about the downfall of the last 'independent' Ukrainian government and the establishment of Soviet power in the region, lasting until 1991.

Virtually by definition, the internationalist parties in Ukraine were dominated by Russians, together with Jews who would not have been comfortable in any expressly nationalist party. Whether before or after the Revolution, when Jews in Ukraine abandoned traditional Jewish culture they invariably adopted Russian rather than Ukrainian norms. While countless Ukrainian villages had a

Jewish population, Jews were mostly to be found in the large towns, which were otherwise populated predominantly by Russians or russified Ukrainians, the Ukrainian peasants living overwhelmingly the villages. When the Ukrainians raised the cry for independence, they resorted almost automatically to anti-Semitic slogans, claiming that the Jews were in favour of rule from Moscow. The Civil War, which tore Ukraine apart and wreaked appalling damage on the population, also saw the worst anti-Jewish pogroms in Russian history. Half a million Jews were left homeless and the number of those who died was in excess of 150,000, or ten per cent of the Ukrainian Jewish population.

In addition to these horrors, the Jewish population of the area saw its economic base destroyed by Bolshevik policy. Under the new regime's economic policy of 'War Communism', as private business and small industry of all kinds were outlawed, a great part of Jewish economic life was reduced to nearly nothing: it has been estimated that between 1918 and 1921 up to 80 per cent of Russian Jews had no regular income. The Conventionists who came to the Black Sea region found themselves engulfed in the full complexity of the Civil War. By coincidence in harmony with shrill anti-Bolshevik propaganda, White politicians in the Crimea were pumping out anti-Semitic hatred in a range of newspapers, principal among which was *Tsar-Kolokol* (The Tsar-Bell). It was this agitation which provoked countless Jews to escape to Palestine and elsewhere, abandoning their possessions and getting out before the expected pogroms. The message was one the Russian Jews had heard many times before, invariably when Russia was in crisis. Now, also not for the first time, it was being proclaimed most virulently by Russian Orthodox clergy. One Father Vostokov declared in the Simferopol city council in September 1919, a year after the Tsar had been murdered, that 'Russia has been lost by the intellectuals and the Jews: she will be saved by the Tsar'. The Crimean council passed his resolution naming the Jewish people 'the enemies of Russia'.

It was a simple message for the simplest of minds to absorb: 'Beat the Yids, save Russia!' The Conventionists' urge to leave became as pressing as that of other Russians who crowded the Black Sea towns and ports alongside French soldiers waiting for ships to ferry them to Constantinople. Baron Wrangel's defeated forces comprised the largest category. Out of nearly 150,000 Russian refugees ferried by over a hundred ships to Constantinople in November 1920, 117,000 were Wrangel's White soldiers. Although some were carried further on to cities in Asia Minor, the bulk of them settled down in Constantinople to await either their return to a Russia purged of its present evils, or permanent emigration somewhere more congenial than post-war Turkey.

Wrangel and his embittered troops established themselves in Constantinople where they created the semblance of a government-in-exile and, in the words of a French intelligence officer, 'strutted like an occupying power'. An irritant and an annoyance, the large White Russian force did not endear itself to the Allied missions which were there to administer a defeated country that was itself in civil conflict. For such an open anti-Semite, it was odd that Wrangel had as his financial adviser Grigory Kogan, a St Petersburg Jew, whose brother Elias, 'something of an adventurer', was director of the Russian Asian Bank and living in the Crimea where he was involved in the repatriation of prisoners of war through the Danish and Swedish Red Cross, and also represented the interests of Deutsche Bank. Wrangel invited Elias to become his finance minister, but there is no record of a response.

Together with their baggage the Russians leaving the Crimea brought along their political views and prejudices, and their humiliation. Russian language newspapers, published in Paris, Helsinki, Sebastopol and Berlin, and ferried by Russian ships back and forth between the Crimea and Constantinople, were sold by émigrés on the streets and in the Russian institutions, cafés and night clubs that had mushroomed in the Turkish capital. Though every shade of opinion, from monarchist to pro-Bolshevik Zionist, was represented, what stands out in numerous French intelligence reports was the mood of Wrangel's men, who 'spoke of nothing but the need to make a pogrom in Constantinople, as if they owned the place'.

The conditions back in the Russian south were deteriorating fast. There was insufficient food, insufficient accommodation and a desperate lack of funds. The only relief came from various American agencies, similar to those operating in the Volga region under the aegis of the American Relief Administration set up by Herbert Hoover. Chone Simon and his friends in Ekaterinoslav, starving and diseased and prey to gangs, heard that there was a British mission attached to Denikin's army at Rostov-on-Don, a major railway centre and a journey of several days. The group eventually found the mission and managed to find its commanding officer, one Captain

Walker, to whom they decided to tell the truth about their plight and their desire to return to their families in London. Captain Walker listened with apparent sympathy, but demanded harder evidence than they could provide. He decided to hand them over to the White authorities while he made further enquiries, with the result that they were to spend seven or eight months in Rostov gaol.

Fed on twelve ounces of black bread a day and a little boiling water, one of the men died before Rostov was captured by the Reds and the prisoners were released. When the Bolsheviks found men being held in gaol by Whites, they naturally assumed they must be Red sympathisers, and the Conventionists in Rostov were not about to disabuse them, especially as the Bolsheviks issued them with ration cards. Simon fell ill a week after his release. His former cellmate, a Bolshevik, was now running the local health service, and so he managed to get a bed in the hospital. But after a few days, still seriously ill and for reasons he could not recall, Simon discharged himself. Making his way back to Ekaterinoslav, a fraught journey of ten days in a goods wagon, he collapsed on arrival and remained virtually unconscious for three weeks.

After recovering, Simon spent a little time helping his sister on her market stall, selling anything that might fetch the price of some food, but he was keen to move on. It was now late summer 1920. Together with David Meyers and another Conventionist, he tried doing some petty trade in buttons and bits and bobs in a nearby small town. Then one day they spotted a notice addressed to all British subjects, oil and steel engineers and the like, who were stuck in Russia and wished to return home. Evidently the Bolsheviks were hoping these stranded Englishmen might be exchanged for Russian soldiers in France who had refused to fight after the Revolution and were now interned there. The Soviet government of Ukraine, under Khristian Rakovsky, was using some of its considerable funds for this purpose. Efforts were already being made through the Danish and Swedish Red Cross to assist in the repatriation of prisoners of war, none of which could have been attempted only months earlier, when the turmoil in Ukraine was so widespread.

Since their identity papers stated they were British residents, the Conventionists thought they might as well try their luck with this scheme. The first step was to approach the Cheka for permission to leave the country. The Cheka, or Bolshevik political police, were operating the scheme from their headquarters at Lugansk, almost

250 miles to the east. Meyers, who had lived in England since the age of three and was therefore the most 'British' of the group, volunteered to make the trip to Lugansk. Two weeks later he returned with good news: the Cheka had given permission, but they must first go to Kharkov, almost as far again to the north, where they must see Rakovsky himself. Four of the group, plus one of their newly acquired wives, went to Kharkov where after a week they located Rakovsky and managed to get an interview. They told him they had deserted from the British Interventionist army at Baku. Despite the lack of evidence, they were believed and given permission to leave the country. Simon could not recall whether the Russian wife accompanied them further on their journey. She would not have acquired British nationality by marrying an alien, and whether the romantic Conventionist acquired Soviet nationality by marrying, though a possibility, is unknown.

Reaching Odessa on 1 January 1921, they were allowed to board a British ship, together with twelve other Conventionists claiming to be British. Once on board, they all went to the captain and told him they were not in fact British deserters, but Russians who had returned under the Convention, and that they had families at home in England whom they wished to rejoin. They were allowed to remain on board and the ship set sail for Constantinople. Before landing, the ship was boarded by British military intelligence officers who were investigating reports that there were seventeen Bolshevik spies on board, and naturally the Conventionists were prime suspects. Had they jumped from the frying pan into the fire? Once again, perhaps because of their transparent naivety or the good luck that had brought them this far, they were believed. Like other Conventionists who preceded them, they disembarked on Prinkipo (Prince's Island), an island off Constantinople under British military rule, where they were disinfected, put into a hotel and looked after. On the information available to me, this took place more than a year after any other Conventionists are known to have been in Constantinople, and not many months before the British and other Allied missions would leave Turkey in the hands of Mustapha Kemal.

In Constantinople, a kindly British consular official, one Mr Beaumont, helped the group by encouraging them to write to their relatives in England and posting their letters for them. (Simon's son, Dr Jack Simon, then a boy of seven, recalls a letter from his father arriving in London.) After forty-six days of this gentle treatment, the group were told they were free to go. Wrangel's 'administration', which would not leave the city until 1923, was still operating and was prepared to issue visas for hard currency, and these were attached to travel documents obtained from the French consulate, which, like the Netherlands consulate, was servicing Russian refugees. With money that had arrived from London in response to his letter, Simon was able to buy a passage to Marseilles and on through France to Dover. There, having survived the privations of the last three years, he was turned back because his skin was covered in suppurating sores. Undaunted, he spent three days soaking in sulphur baths in Boulogne, and on the second attempt was admitted back into Britain.

Another escape hatch for Conventionists, who failed to gain access to any other exit, was the French Foreign Legion. When Russia left the war in March 1918, a force of Russian soldiers was taken prisoner by the Allies on the Turkish front. They were given the option of remaining in internment or joining the British or French armies, or the Foreign Legion. If they chose the Legion, they were told, they would receive fifty gold francs at the end of the war and have the right to French citizenship. Some of these blandishments would turn out to be illusory, but for the moment joining the Legion provided a real opportunity to leave Russia.

In the spring of 1919 the Legion was recruiting in Odessa. Many young men who were not attracted by the opposing ideologies of the Reds and Whites chose instead the army which offered nothing but 'Honour and Discipline'. One such was David Kapylov. Born in 1896 in Vitebsk, his family had taken him to London in 1906, and in 1917 he had returned under the Convention. His first plan had been to go east through Siberia from Chelyabinsk, but he changed his mind and instead found his way to Odessa, where in December 1918 he obtained a new Russian passport. Three months later he signed on in the French Foreign Legion, which was probably the only force apart from the Red Army that took no interest in a man's country of origin or his religion. As his discharge book shows, he saw service in North Africa for the next five years, ended up a sergeant and re-entered Britain in 1924. Strangely, perhaps in a moment of absent-mindedness, the immigration official who issued his temporary entry permit at Dover stamped his Russian passport, surely a more problematical document than the Legion discharge book with its evidence that he had served in an Allied force. As a beneficiary of the comparatively relaxed culture of British bureaucracy, Kapylov eventually became a British citizen and remained in England to the end of his long life.

Abraham Zalofsky had finished trade school in Odessa and had been sent to London in 1912 at the age of eighteen 'to train as a geologist', but ended up working in a small factory making uppers for shoes. A twenty-three-year-old married man with a child when the call to arms arrived in the summer of 1917, he chose to go back: 'I wanted to see for myself this new idea of a free Russia and to see my family at the same time.' He had not attended many meetings in London to hear what the agitators had to say, regarding himself as a thinking man who made up his own mind. As a socialist he had been against the war and against imperialism: 'Like every Jew in Russia, I was political.' As a boy in Odessa he had handed out leaflets for the Bund, and he had come to England with an older brother. They went back together, but his brother died in Minsk in 1922, after Zalofsky had left to return to England.

Like the Shukman brothers, the Zalofskys arrived at Archangel in the *Kursk*. Via Moscow, they made their way to Odessa, located other members of the family, and found that their younger brother was in a Red Guards unit organised by their old schoolmates, the Kangun brothers. There was frequent fighting on the streets of Odessa, and Jewish self-defence units which had first been effective in the 1905 Revolution now re-emerged in Bolshevik guise. Another force, the 54th Ukrainian Regiment, was organised by Misha Yaponchik – the 'Japanese', so named because of his slanting eyes – a figure from the Odessa Jewish underworld, a gangster who had been imprisoned after 1905 for bank robberies and who, although he was now fighting against the Whites, was to be shot by the Reds as a 'speculator', or black marketeer. He was the real-life model for Benya Krik, Isaac Babel's hero in his *Odessa Tales*. Abraham Zalofsky joined Yaponchik's regiment, which consisted mainly of Jews, and went to the front where he spent nearly a year.

Soon, various foreign aid agencies began sending teams. Herbert Hoover's American Relief Administration was the largest and most powerful, and there was also the American Jewish Joint Distribution Committee which carried out relief chiefly among the Jewish communities of Ukraine. Zalofsky worked for the 'Joint' as an interpreter and then began to look for a way back to London. He left Russia illegally, using a smugglers' route through Bessarabia, a

Romanian Russian province to the west of the Black Sea, known today as Moldova, where he spent six months in its capital city Kishinev (now Chisinau). There, helped by local Jews, he worked at any odd job to hand. He wrote to his wife and received a reply which he took, together with his tsarist Russian passport, to Bucharest where the British consul issued the stamp for his re-entry into England. His journey overland to the Channel was remembered as 'uneventful', he landed at Dover, got on a train for London, then took a bus home to Whitechapel without further ado.

Rafail Edelman was a twenty-three-year-old powder-puff maker in 1917 when he first heard about the Convention. He knew plenty of young men, whether Russian Jews or British citizens, who had been sent off to fight after only a couple of weeks' training, and he was one of those who firmly believed the rumour that two weeks was about as long as you would live if you were sent to France. Edelman also believed that as long as Russia was in turmoil, by the time a date was set for them to leave and they were all sorted out and arrangements made for each man to be sent back to his place of origin for induction into the Russian Army, months would have elapsed and the war would be over. When he realised he had miscalculated he was surprised by the determination shown by the British government to settle 'this pinprick of a problem' by such a heavy-handed method as deportation. He embarked in the *Kursk* and after a while at sea found himself appointed to the committee, made up of 'revolutionaries and intellectuals', to oversee conditions on arrival in Archangel. He confirmed that the captain of the ship was threatened with revolvers unless he took a group to the city to move things along. After the usual spell in Moscow, he made his way to Odessa where he survived by giving English lessons to would-be refugees, who buoyed their spirits by dreaming of strolling along the streets of London while conversing freely in English. He knew of Conventionists who had got away from Odessa in foreign ships, but he was not among them. Instead, like Abraham Zalofsky, he joined Misha Yaponchik's regiment where he found a couple of dozen other Conventionists who were deputed to guard the Communist Party central committee of the city, and therefore qualified to be described as Red Guards.

In all, Edelman spent about two years as an irregular soldier on the side of the Bolsheviks, but when the famine struck the south in 1920 he decided to move north to the former capital Petrograd, in the misguided belief that the food situation must be better there. Precisely because of the food crisis, in fact, as many as half the population had fled the city between 1918 and 1920. Still, in Petrograd he got a job in a clothing factory as a sewing-machine mechanic, all the time looking for ways to get out and back to England. It was at this time that he managed to establish contact with his father in London who approached the police for help, but without result. His father then went to the Shelter in the East End, a body that had for many years assisted East European Jews when they first arrived in London. The Shelter in turn approached the Home Office and obtained a permit which Edelman's father sent to him in Petrograd. By now, it was 1924, Britain had established diplomatic relations with the Soviet Union and Edelman had a Soviet passport, which together with the Home Office permit got him onto a Soviet ship bound for London. On arriving back in the East End, he reported to the police and was surprised to find they were all too familiar with similar cases of Conventionists coming home to their families and applying for permission to remain. Given that Edelman had no evidence of having served the Allied cause in Russia, in what today seems an inconceivably casual exercise of immigration control, the police merely asked him if he wished to retain his Soviet passport, and when he declined they replaced it with a standard aliens book.

Hyman Lewis was twenty-two in 1917. Despite being a member of the left-wing Herald League, which organised support for the *Daily Herald*'s anti-war stance, in the pro-conscription public mood he had seriously thought about joining the British Army long before he heard about the Convention. But his elder brother had been wounded twice and gassed once in France, and when the Convention was published Lewis signed on to return to Russia. He then changed his mind. But by the late summer of 1917 he was convinced the war would soon be over, asked himself if it was worth risking being blown to bits 'for nothing', and finally decided Russia was the safer bet.

Lewis was one of about 200 men who left Hull on 15 October in the *Tsaritsa*. Just before the ship left, some British officers came on board and asked the men if they wanted to stay and join the British Army after all. One or two accepted. Lewis and his two friends, Abe Kaplovich and Harry Feinberg, also members of the Herald League, decided to carry on and see how things worked out. Lewis had five pounds in cash, a change of underwear and an overcoat. He thought this would keep him going in Russia until he found a job or was taken into the army. By the time they arrived at Archangel, the Bolshevik Revolution had taken place, putting Petrograd and Moscow out of bounds. Hyman Lewis was among those who were eventually sent to Chelyabinsk. He had no problems about his luggage being left in Archangel, as he had only what he stood up in, plus the spare long johns he carried in a small bundle of belongings.

Chelyabinsk was a main gateway to Siberia, a transit point for the hundreds of thousands of migrants who since the emancipation of the serfs in 1861 had been leaving European Russia for the open spaces beyond the Urals. Siberia had figured for centuries as Russia's vast prison camp, long predating the 'archipelago of concentration camps' of the Soviet era. But it was also a land of opportunity. Agricultural land was available for peasants, new factories needed labour, and the usual range of services which expansion and railway-building inevitably create provided jobs by the thousand. Close to the main railway station of Chelyabinsk a separate migrant centre had been built, with its own branch line, a barracks for 1,500 travellers in winter and 2,500 in summer, a hospital, a dining-room, a bath-house for fifty people – divided for men and women. The entire little satellite township is described in the official railway guide as 'clean and sanitarily planned'. Here it was the Conventionists were deposited to await their onward journey. For five kopeks they could take an unsprung carriage into town to buy little extras or for a change of scene. A pawnshop had been opened in town about twenty years earlier, and at least one Conventionist deposited a silver pocket-watch and never had an opportunity to redeem it. Luckily, there was also a synagogue, where a warm welcome and a meal was always available.

Located in the province of Orenburg and set in wooded landscape on the Miass River, apart from some of its churches most of Chelyabinsk's amenities were fairly new, having sprung up with the needs of the Trans-Siberian Railway. Its main street was unpaved and would disappear into a river of mud in the spring thaw, a universal feature of Siberian life. Chelyabinsk linked the European railway system with the Siberian mainline. Described today as 'the old mainline', it would later be by-passed in favour of a more direct link between Ekaterinburg and Omsk. Seventy years after the Revolution Chelyabinsk acquired the title of 'most polluted place in the world', victim of no less than three nuclear disasters, all covered up with characteristic zeal in such cases, until Chernobyl and *glasnost* brought a catalogue of similar catastrophes to light.

But even in the depths of the Siberian winter of 1917, thanks to the migrant centre, the bath-house and visits to the nearby town, life in Chelyabinsk was bearable for the Conventionists. Above all, there was enough to eat. After a few weeks of this comparative tranquility, they were offered the customary railway warrant to go where they wished. The few who opted to remain where they were, some with newly acquired wives, were of course oblivious of the very hard time they were in for when the Civil War arrived in 1919. Feinberg decided to get back to Moscow, and Lewis and Kaplovich chose Kiev. Another friend, Sam Lazarovich, headed for China.

The territory east of the Urals would soon become a vast arena of contending forces, and possession of the Trans-Siberian Railway would be the principal lever of control. In May 1918, a large section of the Czech Legion revolted against the local Bolsheviks and in only one month had gained control of the Trans-Siberian all the way to Vladivostok. The Czech Legion, numbering about 40,000 to 50,000 men, was composed mostly of Czech and Slovak former prisoners of war and deserters from the Austro-Hungarian Army who had enlisted in the Imperial Russian Army, and then been re-formed as the Legion by the Provisional government. After Russia left the war in March 1918, the Bolsheviks agreed the Legion should leave Russia via Siberia for eventual transfer to the Western Front – going east to reach the west. Recovery of control over the railway was crucial to the survival of the Bolshevik regime, and for the next two years the Civil War in the region was fought with that prize in mind. Chinese and Cossack warlords, and Allied Intervention troops, plus the Czechs, were all striving towards the same end, though never in concert. Meanwhile, as the Bolsheviks gradually overcame their enemies in the Russian heartland, so they steadily regained control of the railway, chiefly by the use of Cheka troops. In other words, to have reached Shanghai unscathed, as Sam Lazarovich did, was no mean achievement.

In Kiev, Lewis followed the customary practice for a Jew coming to a strange town: he found a synagogue where he was allowed to sleep on a bench. Kiev was soon to become the epicentre of the Civil War in Ukraine, changing hands as many as sixteen times between Reds, Whites, 'Greens' (bands of peasants and deserters who opposed both Reds and Whites), and a variety of Ukrainian nationalist forces. It also served as the Germans' headquarters when they were in occupation of the territory, and it was as unstable an environment as any for Jews in Ukraine at that time. Whenever Lewis was stopped on the street by any one of the different occupiers, he was saved by the British aliens registration book that he had kept safe since leaving Britain. He had been working in Kiev as a tailor for six months when he and some other Conventionists decided to make a serious effort to get back to England. They discovered they must get to Moscow to obtain the proper authority and a free rail ticket from the 'prisoner exchange centre'. This corroborates what Chone Simon recalled as the arrangement for exchanging British citizens for Russian soldiers in France.

By the summer of 1919 Lewis and Kaplovich eventually managed to get back to Moscow, where they could find no British consul but where instead they found their old pal, Harry Feinberg, royally ensconced in the Hotel Metropole. It is doubtful that, as Lewis claimed, it was Feinberg's Herald League membership card, showing him to be a member of the British Labour Party, that had gained him this enormous privilege, as there was no love lost between the Bolsheviks and the Second Socialist International, to which the Labour Party was affiliated. On the other hand, hundreds of foreign leftist sympathisers, many of them of Russian-Jewish extraction, were turning up in Moscow, making earnest approaches to the Communist Party, and finding the most varied of receptions.

However he had managed it, Harry Feinberg was living in the Metropole, an elegant hotel then and now, a stone's throw from the Bolshoi Theatre and the Kremlin and a place where Lenin and other Bolshevik leaders were occasionally to be heard making speeches. Feinberg (later renamed Fenton) made space in his capacious suite for his friends and they all stayed together in style for several weeks. The time eventually came when they had to get out. In Sam Lazarovich's wake, Feinberg set out for China, while Lewis and Kaplovich found work about eighty miles outside Moscow on a collective farm that had been set up by twenty-five idealists, mostly Russians, but also some foreigners, including an American. The spirit of collectivism was evidently not yet well developed in this commune. The founders were accused of taking more than their fair share, and they retaliated by accusing others, Lewis and Kaplovich included, of not pulling their weight. 'Not wishing to oppose the will of the majority', the two friends left the farm and returned to Moscow.

The Civil War was now in full swing and any approach to the authorities for documentation or support inevitably entailed the risk of recruitment. And sure enough, like many other Conventionists, Lewis and Kaplovich soon found themselves in the Red Army, in an international brigade, where they mingled with Czechs, Austrian ex-prisoners of war and Germans. The unit was dispatched north along the railway towards Archangel to keep the line open. Ironically, this northern territory, which was perhaps the least active of all the fronts of the Civil War, was the one region where British Intervention forces exchanged fire with the Red Army. By the spring of 1920, Lewis and Kaplovich had somehow become separated and Lewis was back in Moscow, only to be sent off again, this time to the Howitzer Division of 4th Army on the north-western front at Dvinsk where he was to fight the Poles. Many of the Red commanders appear to have been Balts, and Lewis found himself teaching English to the Estonian medical officer in exchange for which he was billeted in the relative comfort of his pupil's quarters.

Lewis, by now familiar with the basics of field medical practice, was given the job of travelling on the roof of a munitions train back and forth to Moscow with medical supplies. As he also had the job of distributing medicines piecemeal along the front by horse and cart, he frequently found himself close to the German border on the Baltic. One day, under enemy fire, he abandoned his horse and cart and sought refuge in a village on the road towards Königsberg (Kaliningrad since 1946). The Germans there told him he should give himself up and join 30,000 other Russians in a prisoner of war camp nearby. Life in Russia during the Civil War seemed cheap to Lewis, hardly less cheap than the Western Front, and so he took this opportunity to demobilise himself and to spend some time as a Soviet prisoner of war in German hands.

At this point, Lewis's future wife Betty entered the story, and the interview. She had been working as a secretary in the offices of the Zionist Federation in London, and one of her jobs was to locate Jews in distress, bring them to Britain and send them on their way to Palestine. Betty had a boyfriend in the office who had been receiving requests for reading material from a certain Hyman Lewis in a German prisoner of war camp, and Betty started sending him books. A correspondence between the secretary and the prisoner of war developed, in due course she put his name forward to an agency that was negotiating the repatriation of Jews, and after six months in the camp he returned to England, where he and Betty were married. Once resettled, Lewis sought out all his old Conventionist pals, including Harry Feinberg and Sam Lazarovich who had travelled through the whole of Siberia and Manchuria, reached Shanghai and got themselves back to Britain as general hands in a tramp steamer.

The novelist, Emanuel Litvinoff, had a very sad tale to tell about his father, Max. The story was first related by an eye-witness, Max's friend and next-door neighbour in London, Alex Roitman, whose daughter, Sylvia, was married to Emanuel's younger brother, the historian Barnet Litvinoff. Max arrived in London from Odessa in 1913, his wife following him a few months later, which was quite common practice in those days, and one that had been followed by my own parents. Max Litvinoff was a radical, probably an Anarchist, reputed to have stood on the corner of Commercial Road and Christian Street haranguing Jewish soldiers against fighting for King and Country, quite a dangerous undertaking during the war.

When they heard about the Convention, Max, Alex and some other friends decided to translate their anti-war radicalism into action and at the same time take a look at the new Russia. Leaving behind their pregnant wives and infant children, they eventually landed up in Odessa, the new Mecca for returning Jews, where they survived in what Emanuel described as a freebooting gang, stealing horses and even minting their own money – it could well have been the Kangun brothers' operation. After about a year of life in Russia they decided that, as the south of Russia had become a hot spot of civil strife, Odessa was not the haven they had expected, and they decided instead to make the hazardous journey back to their original port of entry, Archangel. They arrived after the British forces had left, possibly as late as the summer of 1921, by which time merchant shipping was again using the port. They managed to scrape together enough money to buy passage on a ship bound for Britain, but on the morning they were due to sail, Max Litvinoff had not shown up. Neither tide nor captain would wait, but as the ship moved slowly away into the roadstead, Max came running onto the quay. Roitman and his friends watched helplessly as Max's diminishing figure went on waving in despair. For a while, he wrote letters home, asking to be sent warm clothes, food, pictures of the family. Then silence. Emanuel's mother took her children and set off to find out where and how her husband was. Given the dates of Max's odyssey, it is unlikely that, as Emanuel thought, Mrs Litvinoff could have gone to see the Soviet envoy, Litvinov – no relation – since his tenure in London lasted only a few months in 1918. It is more likely that these enquiries were being made after the United Kingdom had established formal diplomatic relations with the Soviet Union in 1924.

Emanuel remembered a barn-like room where a lot of people, clutching 'regulation' packets of sandwiches, were enquiring about their husbands and relatives in Russia. Emanuel recaptures the atmosphere of that fruitless visit in his touching autobiographical account of life in the Jewish East End, *Journey Through a Small Planet*. Eight years after Max had gone back, the family heard he was dead, though they never learnt how or why, just as they never knew why he was late for the ship at Archangel.

Other fathers had been coming home, loud parties and ice cream for the children became a regular feature. As were the sounds of recrimination and tears on the other side of thin tenement walls. For my brother and eldest sister, aged seven and five in 1920, my father's return was forever remembered as a tall, mustachioed figure suddenly appearing, pulling back the bedclothes and tickling their toes (my then three-year old sister remembered nothing). Others recalled a tense, sad time, with the father sending in a neighbour to warn his wife he was back, whether to allow time for his 'deputy' to disappear through the back door, or fearful of an unenthusiastic or confused reception. There were memories of a mother clinging to a strange man's knees, as if never to let him out of her sight again. The children even started playing a street game, inspired by adult gossip, taunting, 'When's *your* daddy coming home?'

* * *

My father David and his brother Israel (Srul in Yiddish) were born in the province of Lublin, south-eastern Poland in Baranow, a tiny *shtetl* of 2,300 souls, of whom 1,300 were Jews. At the tender age of nine my father had been put to work with a tailor in a neighbouring village, sleeping under the work table on cuttings and walking several miles home on Fridays in time for the Sabbath. It is hard to judge how much education he had, perhaps only a few hours at the Hebrew infant school, yet he could certainly read the Hebrew prayer-book, and at lightning speed. At work and at home in London he spoke Yiddish, the lingua franca of the rag trade – even the 'English' girls who made buttonholes picked up quite an extensive Yiddish vocabulary – and four years in the tsar's army had given him a good command of Russian, which he enjoyed speaking with his brother when, after we had moved in 1936, the other half of the family came from their West End flat to our suburban house and garden in North Finchley. Whether in English or Russian, writing was an effort he avoided. A regular reader of the London Yiddish newspapers, he could not read English, but with a Polish-Yiddish accent he was, like my mother, functionally fluent in it.

My mother was born in Simferopol, the small administrative capital of Taurida Province in the middle of the Crimea, nicely located for the production of wine and fruit. It was also the headquarters of VII Army Corps. Over half the population of 62,000 were Russian, who lived in the 'European' half of the town, the remaining part, 'with its narrow and filthy streets' (according to a contemporary guidebook), being inhabited by about 10,000 Jews and 7,000 Tatars. My mother's native tongue was Yiddish, but she had also spoken kitchen Tatar, the language of the bazaar and the water-carriers, as well as Ukrainian and some Russian, all perhaps best described as of 'kitchen' quality.

Left in London with my brother of four and my sister of two, she had her third child, another girl, on 1 October 1917, just three weeks after my father's departure. My uncle's wife – who was also my mother's sister – had her first child in January 1918, only three months after her husband had gone. And why *had* they gone? My father revealed a deep, sentimental attachment to Russia and its fate during the Second World War and my uncle was a vigorously argumentative defender of Communist ideology and the Soviet state until the mid-1950s, but I simply have no idea if they were politically motivated in their decision to go back to Russia in 1917 – though I suspect they believed that Russia offered the better chance of surviving the war. Perhaps, as members of the Ladies Garment Workers' Union and the Jewish Workers' Circle, and completely immersed as they were in the working-class life of Jews in the West End – not as numerous, but no less compact than their brethren in the East End – they were reinforced by anti-war emotion and rhetoric, and like the others they must have debated the issue for months on end. My father had had his fill of war as a private in the Imperial Russian Army from 1902 to 1906, spanning the 1905 Revolution. After a journey lasting thirty-six days from Odessa to Manchuria on the incomplete Trans-Siberian Railway, he had been plunged into the huge Battle of Mukden, receiving a long, deep scar in his thigh in a bayonet charge. He told us he had also had to crawl behind the Japanese lines to cut and bring back several hundred yards of the copper telephone wire – 'the enemy's secret weapon'.

In any event, the brothers had decided that if the choice was between being blown up in the trenches or swept along on the revolutionary tide, Russia seemed the lesser evil, especially if the Russians chose not remain in the war much longer, which judging by the anxious tone of the British press seemed increasingly likely. As for leaving pregnant wives and small children, this was a generation that was accustomed, if not inured, to long-distance and lengthy family separation. Dr Samuel Saks told me how his father, having brought his family from Lithuania to London, would spend long months away travelling between Lithuania and South Africa on business. Lazarus Katsenell, whose father went back to Russia from Glasgow via Hull in the *Tsaritsa*, told me that his wife's father had come to Glasgow from Odessa unaccompanied at the age of twelve and bringing his little brother with him. Emigrants commonly moved in flocks and congregated where they settled, and there were charitable organisations which met them on arrival and cared for them.

My father and my uncle left in the *Kursk* in September and were among those who went straight from Archangel to Moscow. There, on 9 October 1917 (New Style) my father's Russian Army discharge book was stamped with a seven-day residence permit. Did this mean he was expected to be in the army within that time, or out of Moscow, or was it the empty gesture of a bureaucrat who had no other ideas? They were then issued with their rail warrants to Simferopol in the Crimea, where they settled in with their wives' family and began earning a living as they had in London, as tailors. My mother's father, Lev, was portrayed in family lore as a drunken shoemaker, working from dawn to dusk in a cramped cellar beneath the city street and clearing the dust from his throat every so often from a bucket of vodka which he kept under the workbench. In fact, the only long-lost portrait I remember of him showed a rather healthy, robust, handsome, even prosperous-looking gentleman with a fine beard, not unlike Edward VII. My mother's two sisters had left their home, one for London where she married my father's brother, the other to New York with her husband. Their mother had died giving birth to the third daughter and my grandfather had remarried and produced at least two more children, both boys. It was with their in-laws, then, that my father and uncle now found a home.

When Allied ships appeared in the Black Sea to evacuate their troops and any other categories of distressed refugees that could show the proper papers, my uncle, a self-taught intellectual and talented linguist, went to Sebastopol and offered his services to the British as an interpreter. In the summer of 1919, Sebastopol was scarcely less dangerous than Odessa. Allied intelligence estimated there were 70,000 Bolsheviks in the city, and mayhem was the order of the day. But food was plentiful and the shops were busy, though Russian currency had lost all its value and had been replaced with local scrip. Against the odds, the atmosphere was optimistic, boosted by the presence of Allied ships in the harbour. The British had a great need of interpreters and my uncle was taken on. As Captain Darby of the battleship HMS *Temeraire* and Captain Spencer of the seaplane carrier HMS *Engadine* wrote in testimonials, 'he had served as a guide and interpreter and had been of great assistance during the stay at Sebastopol'.

With these papers, in due course my uncle was able to obtain passage for himself and my father for the exodus to Constantinople. The journey of four or five days acquired legendary status as the origin of another of my father's injuries, to add to the Japanese bayonet-scar received at Mukden. At night in the middle of the Black Sea, the ship was struck by a storm so fierce that the captain had to mobilise able-bodied male passengers to assist the crew. Somehow, while disentangling ropes, my father's little finger got trapped and forever after, whenever one of us children asked him why his finger was crooked, he would launch into the dramatic tale of the storm at sea.

Without their British military passes my father and his brother would have found it almost impossible to get onto a ship. Overflowing with refugees and crewed by improvising Whites, vessels of all kinds were steaming away from the Crimea on course for Constantinople. Desperate refugees trying to board French naval vessels found their way barred by unsympathetic martinets who operated an arbitrary system of selection. By contrast, the British gained the reputation of humane and liberal treatment and consequently their ships were even more overloaded.

If getting on board had been difficult, getting *off* the ships and into Constantinople was equally problematic. The French took the view that everyone had to be quarantined. Elderly Russian aristocrats who were used to obsequious behaviour from bureaucrats were sent stumbling down the gangway to the accompaniment of foul language from French sergeants who imagined they could not be understood. By contrast, the restrictions imposed by the British when they handled disembarkation were motivated by the need to protect the teeming city from any more diseases than it already harboured, though there were also political considerations. True to form, the British applied a simple system of processing passengers according to the class they had travelled in. First-class arrivals were excused any physical examination or political interrogation whatsoever, it being assumed that they were bound to be anti-Bolshevik to a man, and without further ado they were issued with clean bills of health and politely assisted ashore. Second-class travellers were examined by doctors and interrogated in civil terms before being released. Third-class passengers – suspect as both the lower orders and potential Bolsheviks – were immediately quarantined and then subjected to intensive and mostly unproductive interrogation. Refugees who like my father and uncle could show an Allied military pass of any sort would have walked on and off the ship with unaccustomed first-class immunity.

How my uncle passed his time in Constantinople, and whether the two brothers were in the city together, I do not know. My father's papers include two stamped certificates, one signed by Captain C. Catforth-Perry, dated 17 June 1919, which states that he was a civilian attached to the Black Sea Labour Corps and had been employed as a tailor in the Army Training Schools; and the other, stamped 3 September 1919 and signed by an illegible lieutenant colonel, Commandant of the Army Training Schools, declaring that he had been employed at the Schools as a tailor from 1 May 1919 to 3 September 1919.

Until the early 1920s, Constantinople was the resting place for the multitudes of refugees who had been brought there by Allied naval ships and anything else that looked seaworthy. Because of its proximity and ease of access by sea, the city also served as garrison-in-exile for the vast numbers of White officers and men who had been brought there when the Bolsheviks were on the point of capturing the Crimea. The idea of going back to drive the Bolsheviks out died hard among the military refugees, and as long as the regiments were able to stay together this hope was kept alive. But in post-war Turkey the Russians, officers and men, not only could barely scrape a living, but also felt the Turkish authorities' growing resentment against their presence. The Russians in general declined into destitution, while the military fell into a mood of melancholy, as the prospect of 'saving' their beloved Mother Russia faded.

For Russians who managed to pick their way through the post-imperial debris beyond Russia's western border, Berlin was an attractive and above all affordable destination, especially if they managed to bring with them convertible valuables, such as gold coin or jewellery. White officers leaving Turkey also found Berlin a congenial alternative to Constantinople. But when hyper-inflation hit the Weimar republic in the mid-1920s, making life almost impossible, many Russians moved on to Prague, where there was already a significant population of Russian intellectuals, a Russian university and other cultural institutions that flourished in the newly independent Czechoslovak capital. Most journeyed further west, to Paris, joining the bewildered Russian nobility for whom the French capital had always been a second home. Artists and writers also felt at home in Paris, and many of them settled there, once they realised that in the Soviet Union they were expected to be creative at the Communist Party's behest. An association of Russian naval officers continued to exist in Paris and to publish a magazine, *Morskoi Flot* (Naval Fleet), well into the 1950s. But along with the various 'free Russia' émigré organisations formed in the aftermath of the Second World War, the Russian institutions in Paris eventually faded, leaving little more than a few restaurants and the cathedral in Rue Daru. London also became home to a smaller Russian community, while China, Hong Kong and San Francisco would absorb substantial colonies of Russians who had chosen the eastward path of escape.

My father occasionally reminisced about his time in Constantinople, and for years he used the large leather wallet inscribed in Ottoman Turkish that he had bought in the central market and passed on to me. Although with good reason he often bemoaned the financial insecurity of the tailor's life, he was convinced that his skills had helped him survive the years in Russia, the uncertain time in Constantinople – his commanding officer was 'the best-dressed man in the garrison' – and a period in Paris on his way back home.

David Shukman's tattered army discharge book, showing his service in the Russo-Japanese War, served to obtain a beautifully inscribed laissez-passer, in French, from the Netherlands consulate in Constantinople dated 10 September 1919, for which he paid '100 roubles, five florins or ten pounds Sterling', and which enabled him to leave Constantinople. Marked as valid for travel by sea to London, the laissez-passer got him passage in a French troopship as far as Marseilles. He then made his to Paris, found some cheap lodgings in the district of Charenton, got work in the garment district and tailored long enough to scrape together the fare for the final stage of the journey, which he made on a collier that he boarded somewhere on the French coast. The reverse side of the illegible lieutenant colonel's letter is clearly stamped by the immigration officer at Swansea and dated 12 March 1920. It had taken my father exactly six months to make the journey home from Constantinople. He would remain stateless all his life, always able to find a higher priority for the £5 naturalisation fee. His alien's certificate of registration issued in 1920 records that he had served in the Russian Army in 1905–06 and 1917–20, the first date inaccurate and the second over-imaginative. However, the crucial entry reads, *Passport or other papers as to Nationality and Identity,* 'Military Pass issued by Commandant Army Training School, 3-9-19'.

Among the Conventionists were many who went back to witness a tsar-free Russia, and if possible to participate in the thrilling prospect of building a new life on socialist principles. Anti-war views and socialist ideas were well entrenched among the Russian Jews. The impact of the Conventionists' departure was felt, for example, in the various tailoring unions and political circles to which they belonged, and was lamented by organisers and Labour politicians alike. The ideological motivation in returning to the land of the Revolution, even if also to avoid military service, is not to be doubted. Though most men in the category of the politicised were young and unmarried, it is also true that among the married men were some who planned, or hoped, that their wives and children would be able join them in Russia.

It appears that as many as 2,500 of the men who went back were single. As for the families, it is impossible to know the attitudes of wives: whether the prospect of waiting, often penniless, for a husband to return from Russia was better or worse than waiting to hear that he had been killed in action in France. Most of the married Conventionists intended to return to Britain when the war was over and the dust had settled over their contentious behaviour. Some of them had been conscripted into the Russian Army in the dying days of the Kerensky regime, although how many, when or where is not recorded in Russian military archives. A group of seventeen Russian

Jewish soldiers, who had been prisoners of war in the hands of the Germans and were stranded in Rotterdam, would successfully claim the right of re-entry into the British Isles in 1919 on these grounds. The accounts of how men re-entered Britain, though few and unrepresentative, are much more varied than those describing their departure. Good and bad luck, an ill-informed immigration official, a sympathetic ship's captain, a scrap of paper, even unstamped – these and many others were the haphazard elements of a man's success or failure in his efforts to rejoin his family in Britain.

Epilogue

Zeppelins, beautiful silver pencils in the sky, started dropping bombs on London in 1915 and were still doing it in 1917. Conventionists' wives, feeling doubly abandoned now, followed their established routine, grabbing their children and rushing to the nearest Underground station. From Hanson Street, where my mother was living, the dash to Goodge Street station in Tottenham Court Road was a matter of minutes. With a small boy of four, a tiny girl of two at her feet and a baby in her arms, my mother ran like everyone else, bewildered by the lot that had befallen her, but driven by the instinct to save her children and herself.

All the time her husband was away she worked at home, finishing jackets for my father's former employers in Savile Row, while the children played on the stairs or in the street, safe then from any traffic apart from the occasional horse-drawn van or cart. Addressed by my father variously as Manya, Masha or Marusya, all Russian derivatives of Maria or its Hebrew form Miriam – and rendered in her aliens registration book as Minnie – she was used to work, having started in Simferopol when she about twelve. But now, aged only twenty-five and the mother of three small children, she was in a foreign country without her husband. She had come to London only four years earlier, had disembarked with her bundles – and hidden in them her first child, a baby boy of three months, my elder brother Nathan – thinking Wapping to be New York, where her younger sister, Rosa, was living. My father, who had arrived a few weeks earlier, brought her to Soho, where his Aunt Polina had lived since the 1880s or 1890s. Four years, three children and several different abodes later, she was now alone.

Or rather she had been *left*, for it was difficult in that environment to be truly alone. Certainly, the East End, with the greatest concentration of Russian Jews in England, offered a degree of solidarity and familiarity on a larger scale than the West End. But the area north of Soho around Middlesex Hospital, bordered by Oxford Street to the south, Marylebone Road to the north, Great Portland Street and Tottenham Court Road to the west and east – and, as it happens, surrounding the Communist Club in Charlotte Street – belonged substantially to the smaller West End Jewish community. Several synagogues catered to rich and poor, the older German and Sephardic families and the more recently arrived Polish and Russian immigrants.

Around the corner was my mother's sister, Bessie, who had come in 1914 to marry my father's younger brother, Israel. She too was expecting a child, her first, in January 1918 and, also a tailoress, she would have to cope without her husband. Across the road was Mrs Foster who never recovered from the horror of seeing her husband killed in the 1905 pogrom in Odessa, and who had escaped to London with her children. One of them, Teddy, would go on to support the family as a popular trumpet-playing bandleader in the 1930s. There was Mrs Fishbone (Fishbein), whose husband had also gone back to Russia, and Dora Rock, a woman whose size and dependability justified her name, and many others. Like their men, who clung together as they struggled to survive in revolutionary Russia, the wives would also maintain a strong bond of solidarity. Yiddish was for most of them their only language: it would take the encouragement of their children – and their children's schoolteachers – in the 1920s to make them tackle English. Dressmaking and tailoring were the customary means of earning a living.

Although Russian Jews of my parents' generation are most commonly thought of as city folk, and were in fact legally classified in Russia as 'town-dwellers', it is as well to note that most of them came from tiny villages – *shtetls* – deep in the countryside, and that they expressed a kind of modified peasant culture: group-minded, uneducated, superstitious. Think only of Tevye the Dairyman in Sholem Aleichem's stories, popularised as *Fiddler on the Roof*. How many of my mother's friends and neighbours, then, would have been capable of reading the Yiddish press, let alone the English newspapers, where they might have spotted the small print announcing that the government had agreed to pay them a 'separation' allowance of 12s 6d (62.5p) a week per wife, and 2s 6d

(12.5p) for each child? The evidence suggests very few in the early years.* Often short of money for the rent, many would more than once have to bundle their possessions – the most valuable being the Singer sewing machine – onto a borrowed fruit-vendor's barrow and, with the tiny tots perched on high, escape in a 'moonlight flit' to other lodgings. It was a precarious existence, but it always had been, whether in Russia or in Britain and even when the men were there to support their families. The absence of news from Russia, as the weeks became months and then years, made life all the more insecure. Was he alive, would he come back? When?

But why had he gone? Why did these men, so many of them having barely arrived in Britain, suddenly, within a couple of summer months, decide to go back to Russia? Many more of their number had joined the British Army, others were doing war work or were exempt for medical reasons. There were also rumours about men who had gone into hiding, afraid to go into the street in case a policeman asked questions. And others were known to have run away to Ireland or the south coast.

Russian Jews had an instinctive wariness of the police that had been imbibed in Russia, where policemen were generally regarded as hostile monitors of public conduct, rather than protectors of the law-abiding citizenry. The contrast with the 'bobby on the beat' could hardly be greater. In Britain the police were unthreatening, and the British on the whole were a friendly lot. As long as one could find work, life was a big improvement on what it had been 'at home'. Then, suddenly, an atmosphere of panic and uncertainty had erupted and the once busy, self-absorbed community had been traumatised by the departure of many of its men, either to the Western Front or to Russia. For a year there had been talk about the war and how it would affect them. One moment the men were to be called up to fight, the next they were not. Were they citizens, what was an alien, were they refugees or immigrants? What was the right of asylum? The street corners and social clubs had buzzed with debate and now, in the summer of 1917, the bubble had burst and a choice had been made.

The evidence of official papers, interviews, press and other secondary material, shows that although questions of maintenance

---

* Only men with wives and children were mentioned, perhaps in the expectation that the only son of a widow would either obtain exemption or join the British Army and receive the usual allowance.

and what was to happen to the dependants of the Conventionists were discussed in parliament and government departments (e.g. Local Government and Health), practically nothing was organised, and what little was arranged was not communicated either clearly enough or widely enough to the families.

The wives lived in almost total ignorance of what had happened to their men. The occasional letter that did arrive gave little hope that the man himself would soon follow. One husband eventually wrote to his wife that a catastrophe had occurred soon after his arrival in Russia. A twenty-two-year-old who had lived in London for only three years, he had gone back with a cousin and a friend. Standing in a crowd of Conventionists on the railway platform at Archangel, the friend got a shove in the back, went under the moving train and was killed. The letter was written in English – 'If he could spell "catastrophe", somebody else wrote it for him', his daughter told me. But while some mail did arrive in England, there is no evidence that any letters got back to Russia during the first year or so. The wives and children of political émigrés had accompanied their men on their return to Russia, but the government had never seriously contemplated allowing Conventionists' families to do the same.

Meanwhile, the wives survived from day to day. About 3,500 men had gone back to Russia, leaving behind more than 1,000 wives and 1,700 children in London alone. These figures are subject to an unknown degree of error, since they reflect only those women who eventually sought assistance, and none of my informants claimed ever to have heard a word about this or any other scheme. Nevertheless, several hundred wives had received support at some time. The fall in their numbers may indicate that half the husbands had come home.

With the Bolshevik regime appearing to have survived the Civil War, the British government assumed that most of the men who might come back had already done so, and it was therefore keen to terminate its support of the families, or, as a first step, to ensure that none of the families whose father had returned to Britain should continue to receive benefit. A committee was formed in the spring of 1920 to assess the situation throughout the country. It found that 414 wives and 852 children were registered as getting the allowance. By the summer, these inquiries having awoken the rest of community to their unclaimed benefits, the numbers had risen to 639 wives and 1,145 children in London, 27 and 63 in Manchester, and 12 and 14 in Leeds– a total of 678 wives and 1,222 children. These figures confirm the impression that most wives had been unaware that they were entitled to maintenance. To sweeten the pill of imminent termination and to avoid accusations of harsh treatment, the government first raised the allowance from 12s 6d to 15s 6d per week for a wife and doubled the child allowance to 5s. By May 1921, assistance to 238 families had been terminated, and of these only 134 fathers had come back from Russia.

A further statistic that it might have been fruitful to pursue, had there been any other evidence, is that 58 dependants were dropped from the list because they had been 'repatriated to Russia', while a further seven had emigrated 'on their own accord'. Since these figures concern only Conventionists' dependants, we must assume that 65 wives and children somehow managed to get themselves to Russia, presumably during the Intervention when Allied ships were sailing to the south of Russia and Allied military missions, British and French, were somewhere to hand. The only compelling evidence that this happened came from one interviewee.

Abraham Zalofsky recalled that he spent a year in Misha Yaponchik's regiment, taking part in street fighting against various Ukrainian forces in Odessa. The group dispersed when the Bolsheviks were temporarily pushed back in 1919, the year when the new regime itself thought it was hanging by a thread. One day, he was sitting in a café when his young sister came running, calling out 'Your wife is here!' His wife, as he related it, had been brought with their little girl in a British warship to the Black Sea port of Novorossiisk, where Allied forces were grouped, and had found her way to Odessa, expecting to settle in Russia with her husband. But conditions were so bad, food in such short supply, violence on the street so widespread – though, ironically, it was thanks to Jewish self-defence groups that Odessa was the only city in Ukraine where pogroms did *not* take place at that time – that he decided to get her and the child out. His wife was British-born and therefore entitled to the care of local British officials, whereas Zalofsky had to resort to a bumpier path of return. After working with the American Relief Administration, he smuggled himself into Romania, presented himself to the British consul and on the basis of his work for an Allied agency got a visa, travelled to Belgium where the Jewish community helped him get in touch with his family and, with no difficulty at Dover, made his way back to the East End. How did his

British wife fare when she arrived back at a British port, minus the husband she had gone to join? Did his papers indicate that he had a British-born wife? Like much of the Conventionist story, the details are tantalisingly absent.

* * *

In the aftermath of the war, the drastic change in the international climate exposed the Conventionists' 'plan' – to go back to Russia, wait for the end of the war and then return home to Britain – as increasingly unrealistic. Lenin's seizure of power and the separate peace he signed with Germany only a few months later, were seen by the British Establishment and most of the press as a betrayal of democracy and 'a stab in the back'. Inside Russia these acts soon also aroused a broad, if loose, alliance of White forces who for a moment in 1919 were close to bringing the Bolshevik regime down. The Allies responded to the White appeal for assistance, and for nearly three more years Russia was torn by the Civil War. But the armies and the organised workers of the West were reluctant to go on fighting, especially against the 'first workers' state', and the Intervention achieved little and fizzled out. By the spring of 1920 in European Russia and 1922 in Siberia, foreign forces had been completely withdrawn and Lenin's Communist government was firmly in power.

By this time, though welcomed by many in the West, the Soviet regime was seen as iron-fisted, cruel and pitiless. In July 1918 the Tsar and his entire family were murdered in cold blood, and other atrocities committed by the 'Red Terror' were given wide publicity in the Western press.

In March 1919 Lenin launched the Third (Communist) International, or Comintern, an organisation of dedicated activists whose task was to lead the workers of the world to overthrow their governments and make Bolshevik-style revolutions of their own. Communists from all over the British and French empires were encouraged and given material help by their comrades in Moscow to use all means to attack imperialism and gain their independence.

The Bolshevik Revolution of 1917 did not immediately render the Convention invalid. Russia left the war, but Britain and the other Allies would continue fighting for another year. Maxim Litvinov had barely taken up his post as the Soviet government's envoy in London in February 1918 when he wrote to the British foreign secretary to complain that Russian citizens in Britain were still being forced 'to enter the Army and take an active part in a War in which their country no longer participates, having entered into negotiations for peace'. With what Special Branch knew of his record in Britain during the war, it was surprising that Litvinov was ever allowed to re-enter the country, let alone represent Soviet Russia, and he was duly arrested as a troublemaker and deported ten months after his arrival. Meanwhile, the government decided to stop coercing the Russian Jews, the fruits of the policy plainly not being worth the trouble.

It was bad luck for Conventionists wanting to come back to Britain that many prominent Bolsheviks were of Jewish origin, as part of the British press was popularising the view that the entire Bolshevik Revolution was nothing more than a German-Jewish plot to take over the world, starting with Russia. A new Aliens Bill which became law at the end of 1919 greatly toughened earlier provisions to prevent the entry of 'undesirables'. The debate on this bill made it plain that the target of these new measures were the Russian Jews who were seeking to re-enter the country 'after having waited out the war in Russia'.

Russian Jews who had refused to serve in the British Army were seen as anti-British and therefore pro-Bolshevik, as many indeed were, even if their desire to help build the new society was outweighed by the more urgent desire to get back to Britain and their families. The virulently anti-Bolshevik press blamed foreign-born Jews as the instigators of revolution in Britain. *The Times* was to play a particularly important, and somewhat contradictory, part in this period. In 1920 it was the first British newspaper to publish, and in 1921 the first to expose as a forgery, the *Protocols of the Elders of Zion*, a document concocted by the Russian secret police in 1897 and published in 1903 on the eve of the Odessa pogrom and again in 1905, and purporting to prove the existence of a Jewish conspiracy to take over the world. Although the Provisional government under Alexander Kerensky ordered its destruction, it was reprinted in 1917 and at frequent intervals and in many languages thereafter as the handbook of anti-Semites and conspiracy theorists.

One effect of the First World War was that latent hostility to foreigners and foreign residents erupted in Britain, as in many other free countries. Demobilised after four years of largely inglorious misery fighting for King and Country, and returning home to face unemployment and poverty, ex-soldiers were in no mood to tolerate aliens who had evaded war service and who seemed to expect life to go on after the war as though nothing had happened. Apart from such newspapers as the *Manchester Guardian* and opposition voices in Parliament, the government seemed to reflect the general mood of the public.

Well before the signing of the Convention, the attitude of the British government, and much of public opinion, had been hostile to 'friendly aliens' who chose not to join the British Army. The government body responsible for deportations and refugees, the Whitehall Aliens and Nationality Committee, pursued the policy of 'refusing to receive back Russians who had left the United Kingdom under the ... Convention', and it took the view that their dependants should also be shipped back to Russia when possible. This hostility was noticeably moderated when the case concerned a Russian Jew who could show that he had served in an Allied force, for example, the Russian Army under the Provisional government, or one of the units set up by the British or French military missions. Hence the value of a letter of recommendation from a British officer in the field. It also appears that those who met the harshest reception from His Majesty's authorities were men who had grown up in England, appearing the 'most British', while anyone who had arrived here shortly before the war was deemed to have had more cause to return to Russia.

The conscription debate had provoked comment aimed at shaming the Russian Jews into joining the British Army by playing on the themes of gratitude and loyalty, but the most blatantly anti-Semitic press campaign erupted only *after* the war. For anti-Semites, inside and outside Russia, Russia's ills were ultimately caused by the Jews. Whether it was the overthrow of the Tsar or Russia's premature exit from the war or, especially, the betrayal of the democratic revolution by the Bolshevik seizure of power in October 1917 or, most heinously, the murder of the Russian royal family, the Jews were named as the culprits.

In fact, of course, the Bolshevik cause was not a Jewish cause, and anti-Semitism, though common, was not the universal currency of the British press. Nevertheless, late 1919/early 1920 was not the most auspicious moment for a Russian Jew to seek to re-enter the Britain he had left only two years or so earlier as a military 'refusenik'.

And despite the hostile tone of press opinion and the bureaucratic obstacles many returning Conventionists encountered – including some who were never permitted to land, and were deported back to their port of embarkation in France – it is still the case that even those, like my father and my uncle, who retained alien status to the end of their lives, continued to live in England, to work and to bring up their families with the lightest of official hands resting on their shoulders. My father's aliens registration book exercised no more onerous control than to note any change of address and the date of his retirement, but otherwise his presence and activities went unrecorded. In April 1941 – not a date of any significance I am aware of – we were visited by a friendly Mr Gibbon of 'Y' Division of the Metropolitan Police who, as I remember, sipped his tea at the kitchen table, exchanging pleasantries, and then just before leaving breathed on his rubber stamp and noted in my father's registration book that he was still residing at the address we had moved to in 1936.

Like everyone else, the British-born children of Russian aliens – whether or not their parents were naturalised or remained stateless – were British citizens, holding the same rights and obligations as other citizens. The system hiccupped in my case, undoubtedly because my father had never naturalised and Britain's adversary in the Cold War was the Russia he had left behind in 1919. In March 1951, having taken deferment for my studies three years earlier, I suddenly got a letter from the Air Ministry warning me that, as the son of a stateless Russian, I 'might possess dual nationality, Soviet and British'. If I delayed starting my National Service beyond my twenty-first birthday in March 1952, I might still have a claim on Soviet nationality – a *claim*, were they *serious*? – in which case I would have to go through an official procedure to relinquish it, whereas if I joined up before reaching twenty-one I would automatically establish sole British nationality. I duly joined up that September. For me, this episode provides an elegant closure to my father's story: his relations with the British state had been temporarily troubled by his avoiding military service, while his son's were simplified and regulated by entering the Services. And as an added irony, I spent my two years in the Royal Air Force training to become a Russian interpreter.

Acknowledgements

The initial stimulus to write this book came naturally enough from my memories of my father's own account, and that of his brother. But it was my friend, Professor Barbara Harrell-Bond, the founder and *doyenne* of Refugee Studies, at Oxford University and elsewhere, who convinced me that this is a chapter in Refugee History and urged me to make the effort. I am deeply grateful to her. I started work on the book a quarter of a century ago, but my attention was soon distracted by a succession of other projects which meant laying this one aside.

My son Henry recently persuaded me to revisit my notes, and I thank him warmly for reminding me that his grandfather's experience has a wider significance than my historical interest. Not only did Henry read my manuscript, but he also travelled to Archangel on my behalf, where Professor Mikhail Souproun and Dr Tatyana Troshina received him with courtesy, provided him with much valuable information and introduced him to the less visited areas of the conurbation. I am deeply grateful to Henry and his new friends in that hospitable northern city.

I am grateful to Professors Mikhail Narinsky, Oleg Rzheshevsky and to the memory of the late Dmitri Volkogonov for helping me gain access to archives in Moscow.

To Anton Fenton (the son of Harry Feinberg) I am grateful for drawing my attention to the scrapbook of an unnamed Conventionist in *The Shanghai Weekly*.

And to the late Nicholas Bridges-Adams I owe thanks for the access he generously gave me to his grandmother's papers.

To the late Dr Samuel Sacks I am grateful for the memories of his time as a newly qualified physician in the East End.

To my son David I am indebted for keeping me company at the first of the interviews, and to my wife Barbara I am deeply grateful for her help in scanning the British press of 1917, and for providing an interested and reassuring presence at the interviews. I am most grateful to the Nuffield Foundation for a travel grant.

To José Patterson I am grateful for her useful book suggestions, and to Ezra Spicehandler and the late David Patterson for their kindly showing me their manuscript of Joseph Brenner's stories.

My greatest debt is to the survivors I was lucky enough to find, and who shared with me the often painful memories of a chapter in their past. Without their testimony, and that of their family members, I would not have attempted to write this book. Not all of them wished to be identified, but both to them and to those named in the text I am deeply indebted. They include Abraham Aspess, Rafail Edelman, the family of Samuel Goldman, David Kapylov's daughter Lola Green, Lazarus Katsenell, Harris Levine's daughter Beatrice Linden, Hyman and Betty Lewis, Barnett and Sylvia (Roitman) Litvinoff, Emanuel Litvinoff, Miriam Shustock, Chone Simon and his son Dr Jack Simon, and Abraham Zalofsky.

Bibliography

ARCHIVES

Bridges Adams Papers, included in Chicherin Papers, Bakhmetiev Archives, Columbia University, New York.

British Board of Jewish Deputies.

Central State Military History Archives (TsGVIA), Moscow.

French Defence Ministry Archives, Vincennes, Paris.

Imperial Russian Foreign Policy Archives (AVPR), Moscow.

Mowschowitch Papers/Wolf Archive, Jewish Scientific Institute (YIVO), New York.

Nicolaevsky Collection, Hoover Institution, Stanford, California.

Okhrana (Russian Secret Police) Archives, Hoover Institution, Stanford, California.

Public Record Office (National Archives), Kew, UK, HO45/10818, 10819, AIR 1/39, FO371, HO144/2158/322428.

Scientific and Informational Centre for the Political History of Moscow, formerly Archives of the Moscow Oblast Organisation of the Communist Party of the Soviet Union.

Sokolov Archive, Central Zionist Archives, Jerusalem, A18/30.

NEWSPAPERS

Cotton Factory Times, Ashton-under-Lyne.

Daily Chronicle, London.

Daily Mail, London.

Evening Standard, London.

Jewish Chronicle, London.

Manchester Guardian, Manchester.

Shanghai Weekly, Shanghai, 9 March 1918.

The Call, London.

The Times, London.

Utro, Archangel, September–November 1917.

SECONDARY SOURCES

An Appeal to Public Opinion: Should the Russian Refugees be Deported? (The Committee of Delegates of Russian Socialist Groups in London, July 1916).

Arkhiv russkoi revolyutsii, vol. XVIII (Berlin: Slowo-Verlag, 1928).

Brenner, Joseph, *One Year and Other Stories,* translated from Hebrew by David Patterson and Ezra Spicehandler (New Milford, CT: The Toby Press, 2006).

Carsten, F.L., *War Against War* (London: Batsford, 1982).

Ceadel, M., *Pacifism in Britain: The Defining of a Faith, 1914–1945* (Oxford: Oxford University Press, 1980).

Cohn, N., *Warrant for Genocide* (London: Eyre and Spottiswoode, 1967).

Diterikhs, M.K., *Ubiistvo Tsarskoi Sem'i i Chlenov Doma Romanovykh* [The Murder of the Royal Family and Members of the House of Romanov] (Vladivostok, 1922).

Druker, Abraham G., *Jews in World War I: A Brief Historical Sketch* (New York, 1939).

Englander, David (ed.), *A Documentary History of Jewish Immigrants in Britain, 1840–1920* (Leicester, London and New York: Leicester University Press, 1994).

Evreiskaya Entsiklopediya [Jewish Encyclopedia], 16 vols. (St Petersburg: Brokhaus and Efron, 1908–13).

Fridolin, Vl., *Voiskam russkogo otryada v Anglii, Frantsii i Makedonii* [To the Russian Troops in England, France and Macedonia] (n.p. March (April) 1917).

Futrell, M., *Northern Underground* (London: Faber, 1963).

Geiking, A.A., *Chetvert' veka v rossiisskoi konsul'skoi sluzhbe, 1892–1917* [A Quarter Century in the Russian Consular Service, 1892–1917] (Berlin, 1921).

Gitelman, Z., *Jewish Nationality and Soviet Politics* (Princeton, NJ: Princeton University Press, 1972).

Henryk Erlikh un Viktor Alter (in Yiddish) (New York, 1951) (for Alter's reminiscences).

Kadish, S., '"Boche, Bolshie and the Jewish Bogey": The Russian Revolution and Press Anti-Semitism in Britain 1917–21', *Patterns of Prejudice*, 22:4 (1988).

Kadish, S., *Bolsheviks and British Jews* (London: Frank Cass, 1992).

Kennedy, Thomas C., *The Hound of Conscience: The History of the*

No-Conscription Fellowship, 1914–1919 (Fayetteville: University of Arkansas Press, 1981).

Kershen, Anne J., 'Trade Unionism amongst the Jewish Tailoring Workers of London and Leeds', in D. Cesarani (ed.), *The Making of Anglo-Jewry* (Oxford: Blackwell, 1990).

Krestovskaya, Lidiya, *Iz istorii russkogo volonterskogo dvizheniya vo Frantsii* [The History of the Russian Volunteer Movement in France] (Paris, 1921).

Leshchinsky, Yaacov, *Dos sovetishe idntum* [Soviet Jewry] (in Yiddish) (New York, n.d.).

Levene, Mark, *War, Jews, and the New Europe: The Diplomacy of Lucien Wolf, 1914–1919* (Oxford: Oxford University Press, 1992).

Levin, Nora, *The Jews in the Soviet Union since 1917: Paradox of Survival*, 2 vols. (New York: New York University Press, 1988).

Litvinoff, Emanuel, *Journey Through a Small Planet* (London: Michael Joseph, 1972).

Lloyd George, David, *War Memoirs* (London, 1942).

Lobanov-Rostovsky, N.B., *The Grinding Mill: Reminiscences of War and Revolution in Russia, 1913–1920* (New York, 1934).

Maisky, Ivan, *Journey into the Past* (trans. from Russian) (London, 1962).

Nabokov, Constantine, *Ordeal of a Diplomat* (London, 1921).

North-East Lanark Gazette, 18 January 1918 (cutting in National Archives).

Pares, Bernard, *Day by Day with the Russian Army, 1914–15* (London: Constable, 1915).

Pares, Bernard, *The Fall of the Russian Monarchy* (London: Cassell, 1939).

Pinkus, B., *Jews of the Soviet Union* (Cambridge: Cambridge University Press, 1988).

Protokoly zasedanii Vremennogo Pravitel'stva [Minutes of Provisional Government Meetings] (Petrograd, 1917).

Rashin, A.G., *Formirovanie russkogo rabochego klassa* [The Formation of the Russian Working Class] (Moscow, 1958).

Redlich, Shimon, *War, Holocaust and Stalinism* (Luxembourg: Harwood Academic, 1995).

Reiss, Tom, *The Orientalist* (New York: Random House, 2005).

Rodgers, M., 'The Anglo-Russian Military Convention and the Lithuanian Immigrant Community of Lanarkshire, Scotland, 1914–1920', *Immigrants and Minorities*, 1:1 (March 1982).

Rogger, Hans, 'The Jewish Policy of Late Tsarism: A Reappraisal', *Wiener Library Bulletin*, vol. XXV, nos. 1 and 2, new series nos. 22 and 23 (London, 1971).

Schillinger, R., 'Recrutement et Moral des Troupes Russes en France (1917–1919)', *Recrutement, Mentalités, Societés* (Montpellier: Centre d'Histoire Militaire et d'Etudes de Defense Nationale, 1974).

Sergeant Clark's poem 'Archangel', <http://mariah.stonemarche.org/poetry/archangel.htm>.

Shlyapnikov, A., *On the Eve of 1917: Reminiscences from the Revolutionary Underground* (trans. from Russian) (London: Allison & Busby, 1982).

Shukman, H. (ed.), *The Blackwell Encyclopedia of the Russian Revolution* (Oxford: Blackwell, 1988).

Shvarts, P., *Leksikon fun der naier yidisher literatur* [A Lexicon of New Yiddish Literature] (in Yiddish), 2 vols. (New York, 1956).

Solomon, Flora and Litvinoff, B., *A Woman's Way* (London: Simon and Schuster, 1984).

Stein, Leonard, *The Balfour Declaration* (London: Vallentine, Mitchell, 1961).

Szajkowski, Z., *Jews, Wars, and Communism*, vol. 1 (New York: Ktav, 1972).

Tsereteli, I.G., *Vospominaniya o fevral'skoy revolyutsii* [Reminiscences of the February Revolution], 2 vols. (Paris and The Hague, 1963).

Wildman, Allan K., *The End of the Imperial Russian Army*, 2 vols. (Princeton, NJ: Princeton University Press, 1980).

Williams, J., *Mutiny 1917* (London: Heinemann, 1962).

Wilton, R., *The Last Days of the Romanovs* (London, 1920).

Wolf, L., 'Russian Jews and Military Service, a strictly confidential memorandum', National Archives.

Wolfe, B.D., 'The Bolsheviks in Paris, August 1914', *Russian Review*, no. 20 (1961).

Index